ENDORSEMENTS

"Grounded in years of experience and one of the most networked leaders within the Asian American Christian community, DJ Chuang offers a primer on the current state of Asian American ministry and brings much needed attention to the changes needed in order to engage the future. A must-read practical guide for leaders hoping to serve in Asian American contexts!"

 –Tom Lin, President/CEO of InterVarsity Christian Fellowship, intervarsity.org

"DJ has done us a great favor by writing this insightful and innovative book. It will challenge and equip you to reach, teach, and release the church to be the beautifully diverse bride that Jesus has created and empowered her to be."

 –Derwin L. Gray, Lead Pastor of Transformation Church and Author of *The High Definition Leader: Building Multiethnic Churches in A Multiethnic World*, derwinlgray.com

"MultiAsian.Church offers insights and foresights that only a seasoned participant in and thoughtful observer of Asian American Christianity like DJ Chuang could provide. By bringing together scholarly works and personal observations of Asian American church realities into one compact book, MultiAsian.Church is the definitive primer for anyone who seeks to advance the gospel among Asian Americans and beyond. DJ has cast a broad, yet unique, vision of "Multi-Asian" congregations, i.e. churches with the cultural capacity to minister to Asians and non-Asians alike. And he has done so without dismissing ethnic Asian churches or encouraging uncritical assimilation into the white evangelical mainstream. Throughout the book, DJ gently, but persistently, calls Asian American Christian leaders to step up and fulfill their potential to renew an American Christianity that will inevitably mirror the rich diversity of world Christianity today. MultiAsian.Church is a much needed conversation starter!"

 –Rev. Tim Tseng, Ph.D., Pastor of English Ministries, Canaan Taiwanese Christian Church (San Jose, CA), canaanem.org, and Co-founder and former Executive Director, Institute for the Study of Asian American Christianity, isaacweb.org

"DJ Chuang has had his finger on the pulse of multi-ethnic church development for more than twenty years. Throughout that time, he has informed the growth of the Movement through observation, research, personal networking, and the dissemination of promising practices. In his new book, MultiAsian.Church, DJ provides us with a deeper understanding of the unique contributions and challenges of multi-Asian ministry, and adds to the growing body of literature informing the future of the American Church."

—**Dr. Mark DeYmaz**, Pastor of Mosaic Church of Central Arkansas, President of Mosaix Global Network, Author of *Building a Healthy Multi-ethnic Church* and *Disruption: Repurposing the Church to Redeem the Community*, markdeymaz.com

"DJ Chuang understands the landscape of the church, and can help you understand the hopeful rising tide of multi-ethnic and multi-Asian movements happening right now. He's an expert in the know, and dialed in regarding not just what to know about the future church, but what to do with what we're learning. Listen to him!"

—**Brad Lomenick,** Former President of Catalyst and Author of *The Catalyst Leader and H3 Leadership*, bradlomenick.com

"Are multi-Asian churches different than multi-ethnic ones? What are the implications for ministry in the West, since Asian Americans are the fastest growing racial grouping in the United States? There is no one more qualified than DJ to answer these questions. Let DJ take you on a journey into the multi-Asian church with his decades of both personal and professional experience through thinking, studying, teaching, and living out these ideas."

—**Daniel Im**, Co-Author of *Planting Missional Churches*, Director of Church Multiplication at NewChurches.com, and Teaching Pastor, danielim.com

"DJ Chuang brings a fresh perspective to serve the multi-Asian church. Through weaving together research, previous experiences and practical solutions, DJ advances the conversation for Asians leading well in a multi-ethnic world. Regardless of your ethnic background, readers will gain practical solutions for hiring, consulting, and ministering in a multicultural world."

—**Dr. Kevin Nguyen**, Lead Campus Pastor of Saddleback Church Irvine South and Adjunct Professor at California Baptist University

"Absorb DJ Chuang's latest book, MultiAsian.Church. His challenge to view the Asian American community as Multi-Asian should be engaged by seminaries, denominations and Christian colleges. Latino church leaders have been saying for years that not all Latinos eat tacos, by which we mean that there is wide diversity of cultural, history, linguistic nuance, and food, and that church leaders will build lasting, generative and fruit-bearing partnerships as they learn and respect these nuances. In a similar way, this book helps us all to understand the breadth of Asian American church models and leadership development opportunities. I know of no other writer in America who has gathered as many names, churches, models, in this space as DJ. We met in the early 2000s as bloggers interested in emerging church and focused on reporting our respective ethnic groups. His work with L2 Foundation, Leadership Network, various magazines and networks, American Bible Society and others has afforded him the chance to meet, get to know, and learn about Asian American leaders around the country. It's a blessing that DJ is sharing his knowledge, network and playbook with all of us in MultiAsian.Church. I wish every success to the growth of Thirty Network, a collaborative that will benefit all of us."

> —**Rudy Carrasco**, Board Member of Christian Community Development Association and Past Board Member of World Vision, linkedin.com/in/rcarrasco

"DJ Chuang is the most connected Christian Asian American in the United States! And through his connections and experiences, he brings this amazing book to us. This book is full of facts, figures, history, wisdom, and strategies for the future of all Asian American ministries. This book is a must read! Whenever I have a question about the latest information about anything Asian American, I always contact DJ Chuang. He is my go-to guy! I am sure that after you read this book, you will realize why he should be your go-to guy as well. Thanks DJ for this tremendous resource for not only Asian Americans but all who serve our Lord Jesus Christ and His church."

> —**Dr. Benjamin C. Shin**, Associate Professor of Bible Exposition and Director of the Asian-American Ministry track for the Doctor of Ministry at Talbot School of Theology and Co-Author of *Tapestry of Grace: Untangling the Cultural Complexities in Asian American Life and Ministry*, talbot.edu/faculty/profile/benjamin_shin

"DJ Chuang has written an outstanding book that will interest church leaders and those with a leaning towards ministering to Asian Americans. This well-researched book delves into the fastest-growing racial group today and the dynamics that have propelled the growth of the Asian American Christianity. Chuang coins a new description—multi-Asian—and explores the opportunity and challenges of these churches with a wide diversity of Asian backgrounds. Besides providing a fascinating exploration of church models, this book gives real-life examples of different Asian-American churches and casts the call for new churches to be planted to reach the ripe fields in America. This book will influence the next generation of leaders and multiply the impact of those seeking to influence the future of Asian American culture and bringing them to Christ."

> —**Angela Yee,** Director of Mission and Ministry at Saddleback Church Irvine South and Author of *The Christian Conference and Event Planner*, angelayee.com

"As church leaders in America looking to the future in evangelism, we face certain challenges. My good friend DJ Chuang has given us a great overview and insights into the fastest growing group in our country. While Asian Americans is a broad term covering lots of ground, DJ gives us non-Asians an understanding that is necessary to build the united force of all believers to reach our land."

> —**Dave Travis,** Chief Executive Officer and Chief Encouragement Officer of Leadership Network, leadnet.org, and Author of *Beyond Megachurch Myths: What We Can Learn from America's Largest Churches* and *What's Next: A Look Over the Next Hill for Innovative Churches and Their Leaders*

"DJ Chuang has articulated the unique 'what' of God's story unfolding in the US with keen analysis and data about Asian-Americans. While this book serves to be a much needed resource, DJ has thrown down the gauntlet. Multi-Asian Church is a manifesto for those in Asian-American ministries and a springboard for those exploring what it means to be the church in a global village."

> —**Rev. Laurence Tom**, twitter.com/@laurencetom

"MultiAsian.Church is a must read for anyone serious about investing in the future of the Church. DJ Chuang offers valuable insights about the unique evolution, multi-layered challenges & opportunities, and transformative potential of multi-Asian churches that are often overlooked or misunderstood by far too many."

> —**Charles Lee**, Founder & CEO of Ideation and Author of *Good Idea. Now What?*, charleslee.com

"A must read book for all thoughtful, passionate Asian Americans! MultiAsian. Church serves as a prophetic voice calling for Asian Americans to step up to answer the gaping needs of the times. The way DJ reframed the experience of Asian Americans not as second-class citizens but as a privileged and gifted ethnic group endowed by God and poised for reconciliatory, transformative roles in society is both affirming and freeing. In a simple, unpretentious way, DJ was not only able to dissect the paucity of leadership issues within the Asian American cultural confines among their own ethnic groups, in society and in the churches, he was able to carve out a unique path and define a critical space for Asian Americans to lead and fully participate in. Asian Americans have been made for such a time as this. The call to action is now and the future of Asian Americans is bright!"

—**Alice S. Chou**, Director of L^2 Foundation: Advancing Leadership and Legacy in Asian Americans, L2foundation.org

MultiAsian.Church is an important work in a time where personal Asian American success often overshadows the difficult labor of past and present communal obstacles in developing Asian American spirituality. Very few people I know have the passion and LOVE for reaching lost Asian American souls as DJ Chuang. DJ has an unwavering commitment to the future and development of multi-Asian faith leadership. He was able to take on a personal subject which we feel that we should know and yet we really don't and turn it into a compelling read that I would recommend to fellow Asian American leaders, community leaders, ministry leaders, and those searching for the reason why God made you an Asian American in this modern day and age. If you minister to Asian Americans, this a must read, particularly Chapter 6 of this book. MultiAsian.Church will be my go to guide for many years to come. A heartfelt and brilliant piece of Asian American history and vision for a hopeful outcome in this tapestry called America. Thank you DJ for this labor of love and purposeful life sharing.

—**Paul Wang, Jr.**, Real Estate Developer and Pastor, twitter.com/@paulwangjr

"MultiAsian.Church is a glimpse behind the curtain of what God is doing in the Asian diaspora that has come to the U.S. Through data, stories and personal experiences, DJ shines a light on the path forward. If you want to understand what God is doing today in and through the lives of Asian American Christians, this book is a must-read."

—**Eric Swanson**, Leadership Network and Co-author of *To Transform a City: Whole Church, Whole Gospel, Whole City*, ericjswanson.com

MULTIASIAN. CHURCH

A FUTURE FOR ASIAN AMERICANS IN A MULTIETHNIC WORLD

BY DJ CHUANG

FOREWORD BY DR. RAYMOND Y. CHANG

ISBN-13: 978-1534942998
ISBN-10: 1534942998
First Edition

Visit the book's website at multiasian.church

Published in the United States of America

TABLE OF CONTENTS

FOREWORD

One of the great road trips I took was a drive across the United States from California to Washington D.C. During the drive, I stopped at a monument simply called, "The Four Corners Monument." What makes this place unique is that it is the only intersection in the United States where four states intersect: Arizona, Utah, Colorado and New Mexico. These four states share this common point.

In many ways, this book is like The Four Corners Monument. It is the intersection of several important and essential ideas. It is the intersection of culture and theology, present and future, first and following generations.

As DJ writes, the landscape our nation is rapidly changing. Asians are the fastest growing ethnic group in the U.S. But looking at the Asian American community is like looking through a prism—you get different colors, shades and light depending on which way you look through the prism. This book will give you a multi-faceted approach to what is happening in the Asian American community and church.

It is at this intersection we often ask the question of how to best reach this diverse and fast-growing group. While it is impossible to offer every possible solution, this book is a valuable map that can guide you through finding an answer.

This book is not just all theory; it is immensely practical through the lens of experience, observation and research. DJ skillfully brings it all together to help us look toward the future.

I have known DJ for over 20 years. Our paths have crossed academically at Dallas Theological Seminary, we ministered together at Ambassador Bible Church, and were missional associates in launching Ambassador

Network. We have been friends, co-laborers, and most importantly, partners for the cause of Christ in reaching the next generation of Asian Americans and multiethnic communities.

With great enthusiasm, I am honored to endorse this book. My prayer is that this book will help navigate your journey so that your ministry will become more effective in reaching the next generation.

Dr. Raymond Y. Chang
Senior Pastor, Ambassador Church, ambassadorchurch.com
President, Ambassador Network, ambassadornet.org

INTRODUCTION

We live in amazingly fast-changing times, perhaps the fastest in human history. It was not long ago when modern life in America was three broadcast networks on television. Music that used to be on cassette tapes was being distributed on compact discs (CDs). VCR tapes and rental stores opened up a new sub-culture of watching movies at home (with microwave popcorn, of course). Personal computers came with floppy disks, and dial-up modems connected the masses through networks like AOL, Prodigy, and CompuServe. Yes, I have a confession to make: I grew up in the 80s.

Less than a generation later, we have cable television with 900+ channels[1] and broadband internet connection in 87.9% of U.S. homes.[2] Personal computing has shrunk to laptops and notebooks. Tablets are everywhere, and flat-screen high-definition televisions have replaced the old bulky screens. The technology you buy in a retail store today (or order online) will be obsolete in about two years. And what you're buying in the store today will be finding its way to the recycling center and the landfill two years later.

Most people would find all of these changes very stressful and dizzying. Who can keep up with it all? If you grew up in a time when the internet didn't exist, like me, you may say to yourself, "Why bother?" and just opt-out from changing your lifestyle of technology usage to stay with the comfortable and the familiar.

Today's generation is growing up in a world that has always had the internet; real-time information and answers are always available at our fingertips, whether you're asking Siri or Google. Common words in today's vocabulary did not even exist twenty years ago: texting, email, emoji, hashtags, WiFi, and so much more. Airports today have cell phone parking lots. Food places like Starbucks, Chick-Fil-A, and Taco Bell have mobile ordering through apps so you can order ahead of time and avoid standing in lines. People relate by communicating and connecting on Facebook, Twitter, Instagram, and Snapchat. There are all kinds of other services and conveniences made possible by the likes of Amazon, Dropbox, Uber, Airbnb, and many more.

Here in the United States of America, technology is not the only thing that's changing. The multicultural diversity of American society is also changing faster than ever before. It was 2003 when Hispanic/Latinos became the largest minority racial group, surpassing African Americans. Since 2010, Asian Americans have become the fastest growing racial/ethnic group in the United States. And it is projected that by 2043, the American population will no longer be any racial group majority in the US.[3] And it is into this ever-so-changing society that the churches in the United States are called to be a witness for the Gospel of Jesus Christ.

In recent years, there's a slowly growing number of published books to challenge and equip the church leaders about becoming a multiethnic church in order to be a more effective witness to a multiethnic society.[4] However, there are comparatively fewer resources for equipping churches to do effective ministry among Asian Americans. The need for developing these resources is becoming increasingly urgent.

DEMOGRAPHICS IS DESTINY

Practically every sector of society and industry recognizes the importance of understanding the times, particularly with changes in population and demographic shifts. In education, schools and universities have modified both classrooms and hiring of teachers to reflect the diversity of the students in their community. In government, different community services are created to provide for the needs of different groups. In business, consumers' needs are constantly monitored so that products and services can best serve the growing number of diverse groups of customers in a free-market economy like America's. The saying "demographics is destiny"[5] is often used in the marketing world to describe just how important it is to pay attention to population trends when planning for the future, or your business will have no future.

How should Christian pastors and leaders pay attention to these changes in population? A church's ministry typically serves an entire community from the cradle to the grave, or birth to death. Factoring in people who are moving in (perhaps from immigration) and moving out of a community (with migration being common in the American life), it means every community's population is constantly changing. If the mission of the church is to reach people with the Gospel of Jesus Christ, church leaders have to pay attention to its community's population.

Looking at the whole population of a nation can be overwhelming or irrelevant. If there were a scoreboard that displayed the real-time population of the United States, that may be interesting, but not very helpful.[6] It would be more helpful to look more closely at a specific context or demographic to have numbers that are more understandable (to wrap your head around it) and actionable (for you to do something about it).

INTRODUCING THE AUTHOR

I write this book as a Chinese-American Christian man about to enter my 50s. I grew up in a traditional immigrant family without any religious upbringing, and did not start my Christian faith journey until the end of high school. When I renewed my commitment to Christ at the age of 25, I sensed a call to minister to Asian Americans. I had no idea what that would look like. So I did the one thing I knew—go to seminary. I attended Dallas Theological Seminary to prepare for pastoral ministry. Those years of seminary education were good preparation, but nothing since has been predictable nor strategically planned.

My life of Christian ministry has taken quite a circuitous path. Only by the grace of God, what seemed randomly coincidental was sovereignly guided. I did work in vocational ministry as a pastor for five years: two years of youth ministry at an ethnic Chinese church, and three years as an associate pastor at a multiethnic church plant with mostly Asian Americans. I did as well as expected as a pastor... But who needs an "okay" pastor? I wanted to serve God with all that I have—my skills, training, and gifts, accentuated with my desires and passions.

Subsequently, I found myself working with an assortment of Christian organizations, two that are particularly pertinent to this book's subject. First, I worked with L² Foundation, a private family foundation with a vision to develop leadership and legacy for Asian Americans. Second, I worked with Leadership Network, a place connecting innovators for the purpose of multiplying their impact. Working with these two organizations in the past 18 years gave me a number of opportunities to connect with Asian American Christian ministry leaders as well as innovative churches that are shaping the future for the Kingdom of God.

WHY THIS BOOK

Since 2009, I've had numerous opportunities to share my research and observations of what is happening in Asian American Christianity through workshops and seminars at conferences and churches. I have received positive feedback that my sharing has been helpful to those in attendance and to those that view the videos or listen to the recordings posted on the internet.

It is my hope that the things I've researched and learned about in Asian American ministry developments will be even more useful in a book format. My prayer is for church leadership teams to read it together and discuss its implications. It should create conversations for churches to thoughtfully and prayerfully consider how to make their ministry more effective for the present and future generations of Asian Americans.

I coined the term "next generation multi-Asian churches" to highlight this unique growing group of church communities I've found in my research. I loosely define the term as: autonomous English-speaking churches led by an Asian American pastor that's intentionally or incidentally reaching next generation Asian Americans and other non-Asians.

WHAT'S IN THIS BOOK

This book is all about the unique opportunities and particular challenges specific to doing ministry within the Asian American context. First we will take a closer look at the Asian American population, because church ministry is all about people. Asian Americans are a very diverse racial/ethnic group of many ethnicities, and these distinctives must be considered when preparing for the many opportunities for outreach, service, and ministry.

This book will also review the variety of models most commonly used by ethnic Asian churches thus far. For immigrants coming from Asia to America, these churches have worked faithfully for decades to meet the spiritual and practical needs of its multi-generational, multi-lingual, and multi-cultural community. There are many lessons to be learned from what has worked in the past and what has not.

Lastly, this book will present the growing trend of next generation multi-Asian churches that I have observed during the past 15 years. This new kind of church model is creatively reaching more people in the younger generations, both Asian and non-Asian. Because these churches are agile and adaptable, they're doing ministry in different ways than the traditional ethnic Asian churches. This gives us a picture of what a future of the Asian American church would look like, because currently there aren't many signs for how existing church models will be effective in reaching the fast-growing Asian American population that's on the brink of doubling.

MY HOPE FOR THIS BOOK

There are many complicated issues when looking at the terrain of doing ministry in an Asian American context. Those that have labored in this ministry context already know the difficulties and challenges, even though there are not many safe places where they're articulately examined, untangled, and resolved. I've seen a number of good books already published and research already done on bringing about better understanding, but I've found very few publications that provide solutions with real-life examples.

This book will present my findings and observations from a new kind of church that is effectively reaching the next generation of Asian Americans and non-Asians too in a multiethnic world. I think it can be more helpful to look at the new solutions instead of troubleshooting old problems. My hope is to help move the conversation forward.

It is also my prayer to see this book be a part of the development of the future church in our multiethnic society within a multinational world, for the sake of the Gospel and to the glory of God.

This book was written and authored using web-based tools available to all of us. This book was written collaboratively with crowdsourcing principles by inviting people to read the rough draft in real-time, chapter by chapter, and giving feedback via a comment section. That feedback was considered and incorporated into the book's final draft. The book is being published digitally first and later in printed format via a print-on-demand technology.

To find additional resources and join in the on-going conversations, please go to http://multiasian.church on any web browser connected to the internet.

CHAPTER 1

FASTEST GROWING POPULATION

Asian Americans are the fastest growing racial group in the United States of America since 2010, by percentage rate of growth. According to the U.S. Census Bureau, Asian American population in 2015 was estimated to be 21 million people[7], and by 2050, projected to be 42.1 million people.[8] In other words, the Asian American population will double in 35 years. How can we, the church, be prepared for this explosive growth?

Before we jump ahead and come up with ideas for what we could do to respond, it is important to take a look at the Asian American population for its history, growth, geography, and diversity.

HISTORY

The term Asian Americans refers to American citizens with Asian descent, based on the U.S. Census racial category of Asian, defined as "a person having origins in any of the original peoples of the Far East, Southeast Asia, or the Indian subcontinent including, for example, Cambodia, China, India, Japan, Korea, Malaysia, Pakistan, the Philippine Islands, Thailand, and Vietnam."[9] This is one of five categories used in the U.S. Census: white, black or African American, American Indian or Alaska Native, Asian, and Native Hawaiian or other Pacific Islander.

A census is taken by the U.S. government every ten years to gather population data to support its policies. Taking a census is not particularly unusual, as it was done in biblical times too, even around the time Jesus was born. As the Christmas story is retold every year, the passage in Luke 2 starts with a description of a census:

> In those days a decree went out from Caesar Augustus that all the world should be registered. This was the first registration when Quirinius was governor of Syria. And all went to be registered, each to his own town. And Joseph also went up from Galilee, from the town of Nazareth, to Judea, to the city of David, which is called Bethlehem, because he was of the house and lineage of David, to be registered with Mary, his betrothed, who was with child.[10]

In their own words, the U.S. government describes its purpose for census: "Information on race is required for many Federal programs and is critical in making policy decisions, particularly for civil rights. States use these data to meet legislative redistricting principles. Race data also are used to promote equal employment opportunities and to assess racial disparities in health and environmental risks."[11] However, while disregarding its own declaration, what the U.S. government has done in its policy-making with Asian Americans historically has been tainted with discriminatory injustice. Three of the most notable ones were: the Chinese Exclusion Act in 1882 which prohibited the immigration of Chinese laborers until 1943, the Japanese American internment camps during World War II, and the anti-miscegenation laws that banned interracial marriage until 1967.

In addition to its past history of legislative discrimination, many Asian Americans have a shared experience of discrimination on a personal and societal level. People make insensitive remarks about others based on how they look, talk, or what they eat. I still hear stories from American-born Asian Americans (even into their fifth generation) about being asked the question, "Where are you from?" And when they respond with California or New York, they're asked again, "No, where are you REALLY from?" Or receiving comments such as "Oh, your English is so good!" Whether these racially-insensitive remarks are intentional or not, they are hurtful and wrong.

JUSTICE

The Asian American church is uniquely positioned to advocate for the social justice of our community, as an integral part of our Christian witness in the world as we proclaim the Good News of the Gospel. Jesus described his work of social justice when he read from the Old Testament Scriptures (Isaiah 61:1-2) in Luke 4:18-19–

> "The Spirit of the Lord is upon me,
> because he has anointed me
> to proclaim good news to the poor.
> He has sent me to proclaim liberty to the captives
> and recovering of sight to the blind,
> to set at liberty those who are oppressed,
> to proclaim the year of the Lord's favor."

Social justice is also listed in the short list of three essential requirements God has for all mankind, as it plainly states in Micah 6:8, "He has told you, O man, what is good; and what does the Lord require of you but to do justice, and to love kindness, and to walk humbly with your God?"

Plus, the Christian church has a historical precedence for being active in fighting for social justice:

> In fact, orthodox Christians have long recognized in Scripture a call to defend and uphold the dignity and well being of all persons, especially the poor and powerless. Take, for example, John Wesley, who led prison reform and abolitionists movements in 18th-century England. More recently, evangelical leaders like Ron Sider and Jim Wallis have promoted Christian engagement in anti-war, environmental, and immigration causes...[12]

GROWTH

The Asian American population had grown most dramatically since 1965 due to the U.S. government's changing immigration policies. Pew Research Center explained it as follows:

Large-scale immigration from Asia did not take off until the passage of the landmark Immigration and Nationality Act of 1965. Over the decades, this modern wave of immigrants from Asia has increasingly become more skilled and educated. Today, recent arrivals from Asia are nearly twice as likely as those who came three decades ago to have a college degree, and many go into high-paying fields such as science, engineering, medicine and finance. This evolution has been spurred by changes in U.S. immigration policies and labor markets; by political liberalization and economic growth in the sending countries; and by the forces of globalization in an ever-more digitally interconnected world.[13]

ASIAN AMERICAN POPULATION (PROJECTED TO 2060)

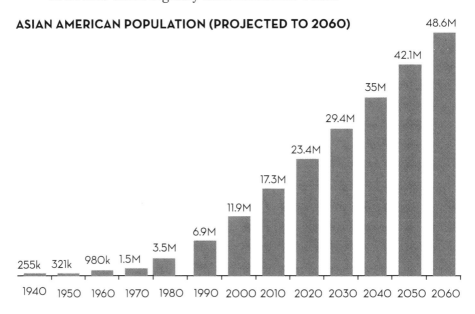

In 2014, the Asian American population was estimated at 20 million. These large numbers are hard to imagine. Let's do some comparisons: the entire population of the entire state of New York is estimated at 20 million in 2014. That's the same number of Asian Americans living in all 50 states!

By 2050, the Asian American population is projected to exceed 42.1 million. Proportionally, Asian Americans currently make up about 5% of the US population, that will almost double to 11% by 2050. On the whole, the American population is projected by 2043 to be multi-ethnically diverse with no racial majority.[14]

How is the Asian American population growing faster than the other racial groups? Very simply, there are essentially two reasons for any population growth: reproduction (typically measured as the birth rate) and immigration. And this shared history of immigration is what a majority of Asian Americans have in common, with 74% of Asian Americans adults being foreign-born.

Even as the economy in parts of Asia has dramatically improved in recent years, many Asians keep immigrating to America. Have you noticed where things are made and manufactured today? Over the past five to ten years, it's as if almost everything I have is made in China: the MacBook I'm typing on, my cell phone, my clothes, my furniture, my kitchenware and so on. Perhaps you've noticed this too. Who would have imagined that China-based Lenovo would buy out the all-American personal computer business brand IBM. And you may recognize these global brands that originate from South Korea: Samsung, Kia, Hyundai, and LG. Not to mention the many global brands from Japan that have endured many decades, like Sony, Toyota, Honda, Canon, Nissan, and Panasonic.

This would suggest that economic opportunity is not the only reason for Asian immigration. There are actually many other reasons for making the dramatic change from one's native country in Asia to immigrate to a vastly different country like the United States. These reasons include family reunification, better educational opportunities, freedom and safety from political and religious oppression, etc. In other words, it could be said that even Asians pursue the American dream.

There's another reason for population changes in a community that should be noted–migration. The population of the United States is considered highly mobile and the Census Bureau collects data on the rate of migration, also known as "geographic mobility."[15] Between 2011 and 2012, 12% of Americans moved at least once. This probably affects you and/or someone you know. One research found that the average American moves 11 times in a lifetime.[16]

Correspondingly, 1 in 8 Americans every year is moving from their current home to live somewhere else, whether moving within their city or county, or moving to another part of the state or a different state altogether. When and where people move have a significant impact on the local demographics and economies of the places where they moved from and where they now live.

This geographic mobility of Asian Americans, whether internationally or domestically, can have a significant impact on the local church. Two things to note here. First, Asians in America are much more receptive to Christianity than their home country in Asia. (The next chapter will take a closer look at the statistics that illustrate this.) Second, people in general are more receptive when they have relocated to a new community, especially a new country. People moving into a new community is a tremendous ministry opportunity for churches to be strategic and intentional in having ministries that welcome them by providing assistance for practical needs of relocating. It is fairly common for Asian churches to provide assistance with language translation, English classes, free legal advice, and other related social services.

Let's take a look at where Asian Americans are living in the United States.

GEOGRAPHY

The chart below illustrates the proportions of where Asian Americans live in four U.S. regions.

The largest percentage of Asian Americans (47%) live in the western U.S. states, with the highest concentration in California and Hawaii. But that also means 53% of Asian Americans live outside of the West, with 11% in the Midwest, 20% in the Northeast, and 21% in the South. When considering where Asian Americans live in regards to a ministry, we should not focus only on the West Coast but see the entire dispersion of the Asian American population in the U.S.

The Pew report also noted: residential settlement patterns vary greatly among different country of origin groups. The West is home to most Japanese-American (71%) and most Filipino-American (66%). Chinese, Vietnamese and Koreans are more likely to settle in the West than in any other region.[17]

In most U.S. states, English is the most spoken language and Spanish is the second most spoken. But notice how many states have an Asian language as the third most spoken language, as illustrated in this chart of most commonly spoken languages besides English and Spanish:[18]

MOST COMMONLY SPOKEN LANGUAGES OTHER THAN ENGLISH OR SPANISH

Did you know that Vietnamese is the third most spoken language in Washington, Texas, Oklahoma, and Nebraska? And Korean is the third most spoken language in Georgia and Virginia? Notice the large Chinese-speaking population in New York and Hmong-speaking population in Minnesota. And there are large populations of Tagalog-speaking Filipinos in California, Nevada, and Hawaii.

What does all of this mean? Here's a couple of thoughts: if a ministry opportunity to Asian Americans doesn't open up in California or one of the other Western states for someone looking to serve this community, there are plenty of opportunities elsewhere in the United States!

And while these demographics have shown the broader distribution of the Asian American population, regionally and state-by-state there are very distinct demographics at a local level. You'll want to research the Asian American demographics for your specific location, whether that's for the city, the county, or the metropolitan area in order to be well-prepared for ministering to this population. Here are 3 great resources for finding local demographics:
- U.S. Census' QuickFacts census.gov/quickfacts
- FactFinder.Census.gov provides census data by state, county, city, or zip code
- city-data.com has aggregated detailed profiles of all cities in the United States

DIVERSITY

Asian Americans are not all alike. Far from it. The many varieties of Asian Americans consist of more than 34 ethnicities, each with vastly different backgrounds of languages, cultures, nationalities, history of immigration, and more. These differences and distinctives are often lost when Asian Americans are grouped together.

For instance, the U.S. Census only specifies these 11 Asian ethnicities by name: Asian Indian, Chinese, Filipino, Japanese, Korean, Vietnamese, Hmong, Laotian, Thai, Pakistani, and Cambodian. And then the "Other Asian" category in the Census would include the likes of: Taiwanese, Bangladeshi, Burmese, Indonesian, Nepalese, Sri Lankan, Malaysian, Bhutanese, Mongolian, Okinawan, Tibetan, Mien, Singaporean, Tamil.

Proportionally, 6 Asian ethnicities comprise 83% of Asian American population: Chinese, Filipino, Asian Indian, Vietnamese, Korean, Japanese. When the Pew report, "The Rise of Asian Americans,"[19] was first published in 2012, it presented statistics on the top 6 Asian American ethnicities that tend to obscure the distinct differences of the other Asian American minorities. The 2013 updated edition provided additional data on 14 smaller Asian ethnicities, with more detailed economic and demographic data for 9 of these groups.

When statistics are presented about Asian Americans, be careful not to use the overall general statistics to describe the whole. 17% of the Asian American population consists of many more smaller ethnicities with very different socioeconomic issues. Therefore, different ministry opportunities require different, fine-tuned, contextualized strategies.

Why is this important? For one, a majority of Asian Americans do not self-identify as Asian Americans. How this preference is described:

> ... the "Asian American" label has not been embraced by any group of U.S. Asians, be they native born or foreign born. Most describe themselves by their country of origin, such as "Chinese American," "Filipino American" or "Indian American," rather than by a pan-Asian label. Overall, just one-in-five (19%) say they most often describe themselves as Asian or Asian American and even fewer (14%) say they describe themselves as just plain American."[20]

Furthermore, to ignore the distinctive cultural differences of this very diverse Asian American population may be racially insensitive or worse, offensive. These racial insensitivities and offenses occur in pop culture when, for example, a fictional character is portrayed with a bad "Asian" accent that is nothing more than mixed-up gibberish. And sadly, insensitive incidents have occurred in American Christianity too. The thing is, unintentional words are just as painful and hurtful in its impact as intentional offenses. Rather than asking the offended why they're being so sensitive, ask why the offender is being so insensitive.

Finally, overgeneralization has perpetuated the "model minority" myth, where statistical achievements by some Asian Americans have overshadowed the serious social and economic needs of other Asian Americans. A statement such as "Asian Americans are the highest-income, best-educated and fastest-growing racial group in the United States"[21] can be mistakenly used to shape policies in governments and ministries in churches that leave the needy in need and the hurting still in pain.

It's true that on the whole, Asian Americans are more educated and have higher median family income than any other racial groups. 49% of Asian Americans have a college degree (or several), compared with 28% for the U.S. population. The educational level of recent Asian immigrants is even higher, with 61% having a college degree. Plus Asian Americans have the highest median household income at $66,000, compared with $49,800 for all Americans. But while a sizeable number of Asian Americans have achieved much educationally and financially, there are also significant numbers of Asian Americans who are disadvantaged and struggling, especially among Southeast Asians and smaller Asian American groups.

Here are a few data points for reference from Asian-Nation's "The Model Minority Image":[22]

- Only 20% of Vietnamese Americans have a college degree
- Less than 10% of Laotians, Cambodians, and Hmong have a college degree
- Almost 40% of all Vietnamese refugees are on public assistance in California
- 40% of Cambodians, Hmong, and Laotians receive public assistance in Minnesota and Wisconsin

And, from the UCLA Asian American Studies Center: 2015 Statistical Portrait of Asian Americans, Native Hawaiians, and Other Pacific Islanders:[23]

- 2.7% of the Asian alone population live in poverty
- 14.6% of the Asian alone population do not have health insurance coverage

THE TASK OF SUB-GROUPING

It is feasible, for the sake of easier understanding and reachability, to aggregate these many ethnicities into three sub-groups for their notable similarities: East Asians, Southeast Asians, and South Asians.

East Asians come from China, Korea, Japan, Taiwan, and Mongolia. One major reason for them to be known as the East Asians is their shared belief and common practices in Confucianism. Confucianism has deeply influenced the East Asian culture and its political life. The desire to have a son, respect for one's parents, respect for the elderly and respect for teachers represent a few of the concepts that arise from Confucian teachings. Confucianism is built on the important hierarchy of five relationships for a harmonious society: ruler to subject, father to son, husband to wife, older brother to younger brother, and older friend to younger friend.

Southeast Asians are from Vietnam, Thailand, Laos, Cambodia, and Vietnam, Myanmar, Malaysia, Singapore, Indonesia, the Philippines, and Brunei. These countries have varying degrees of historical influence from the West: French in Vietnam, Spanish in the Philippines, and China in Singapore and Malaysia.

South Asians are from India, Pakistan, Bangladesh, Bhutan, the Maldives, Nepal, and Sri Lanka. These countries have strong English influences, as they all have been British colonies at some point in history. Desi (a term that describes the people and cultures within the Indian subcontinent) is known for its music and dance, as well as its foods and spices.

BY THE NUMBERS

Here's a breakdown of each ethnicity within the Asian American population by number:

20 LARGEST U.S. ASIAN ORIGIN GROUPS (2010)

All Asians	17,320,856
Chinese	4,010,114
Filipino	3,416,840
Indian	3,183,063
Vietnamese	1,737,433
Korean	1,706,822
Japanese	1,304,286
Pakistani	409,163
Cambodian	276,667
Hmong	260,073
Thai	237,583
Laotian	232,130
Bangladeshi	147,300
Burmese	100,200
Indonesian	95,270
Nepalese	59,490
Sri Lankan	45,381
Malaysian	26,179
Bhutanese	19,439
Mongolian	18,344
Okinawan	11,326

To learn more about each of these Asian American groups, please refer to Section II of "The Rise of Asian Americans" report, titled "Characteristics of Major Asian-American Subgroups,"[24] for an excellent description of each of the top six Asian American groups (Chinese, Filipino, Indian, Vietnamese, Korean, Japanese) with a history of the group's immigration narrative and its characteristics: nativity and citizenship, language, age, marital status, fertility, educational attainment, income, home ownership, poverty status, regional dispersion, and attitudes on life in America.

In Section V of the same report, there are additional tables titled "Characteristics of Smaller U.S. Asian Subgroups, 2010,"[25] with data for 9 more Asian American groups (Pakistani, Cambodian, Hmong, Thai, Laotian, Bangladeshi, Indonesian, Sri Lankan, Malaysian) describing economic and demographic characteristics of the groups.
With so many Asian Americans from different countries, each ethnicity also possesses different religious influence and varying exposure to Christianity. The next chapter will take a look at the faiths and religions of Asians and Asian Americans.

CHAPTER 2
RELIGIOUS ROOTS OF ASIAN AMERICANS

Asian Americans have a wide diversity of cultures, languages and mix of religious faiths and practices. When looking at the religious context of Asian Americans, those that share the immigrant journey have experienced going from an Asian society where Christianity is a minority religion to the Western society where Christianity is a majority religion.

For immigrants that are relocating from Asia to America, religion can be a very helpful resource in absorbing the culture shock and getting acclimated to a new country. For some Asian Americans, this occasion may prompt them to rediscover their family's religious faith. For others, there's an openness to explore Christianity because of the cultural familiarity in an ethnic Asian church.

In recent years, there has been a growth in academic works related to the sociology of religion. There's also a whole line of academic studies for comparative religions. So for such study, I will refer you to other experts for a more in-depth analysis about the theological differences and nuances of Asian religions. These 3 titles are among the best selling books about comparative religions: *The World's Religions* (2009) by Huston Smith, *God Is Not One: The Eight Rival Religions That Run the World* (2011) by Stephen Prothero, and *Nine Theories of Religion* (2014) by Daniel Pals.

This chapter will focus on how churches and pastors can be more effective in ministering to Asian American immigrants with other religious backgrounds. My observations, remarks, and suggestions will draw from my research and my life experiences of working with Asian American churches.

This book will also make extensive reference to 2 reports published by Pew Research Center, "The Rise of Asian Americans" and "Asian Americans: A Mosaic of Faiths."[26] This is the largest research project to date that summarizes the socioeconomic and lifestyle characteristics of the Asian American population using Census data and surveys. Scholars and advocates for Asian American communities have raised serious concerns for the reports' broad overgeneralization and how their summaries misrepresent the very diverse Asian American population, both the tendency of reinforcing model minority stereotypes and overshadowing the needs of Asian American minorities.[27] Recognizing the limitations and the shortcomings of these reports, the research data still does provide a useful point of reference.

POPULAR RELIGIONS IN ASIA

Using the previously introduced framework of 3 major regional groupings of Asians (East Asians, Southeast Asians, and South Asians), here are the commonly acknowledged ideologies, philosophies, and metaphysics that have influenced the faiths, religions, and spiritualities commonly practiced traditionally by a majority of people in Asia.

The East Asian culture has been strongly influenced by the syncretic blend of Buddhism, Taoism, and Confucianism, together known as the "Three Teachings" in Chinese philosophy. Duly noted, that Taoism and Confucianism are more philosophies than religions, while some experts say that Buddhism is more a way of life than a religion. Some religions are more specific to a country: Korea has shamanism, Japan has Shinto, and China has folk religions characterized by veneration of ancestors, spirits, and deities. Wanda M. L. Lee described the influence of the "Three Teachings":

Many Asian cultures are influenced by the philosophies of Confucianism, Buddhism, and Taoism. Among the values that appear common to many Asian cultures are those of harmony; humility; and respect for family, authority, and tradition.[28]

Southeast Asians have influences from many major religions, including Buddhism, Animism, Catholicism, Islam, Confucianism, and Hinduism. Specific religions have been strongly influential in certain countries, for instance: Islam in Indonesia and Malaysia, Catholicism in the Philippines, Buddhism in Thailand and Myanmar. Vietnam's most popular religion is Buddhism with influences of the "Three Teachings" from East Asia.

As for South Asians, a majority practices Hinduism (around 61%) and about 32% practice Islam. Sikhism, Buddhism, and Christianity comprise a small minority that together total less than 10%.

This table shows the religious affiliations of each Asian country in Asia as reported in the CIA *World Factbook*:[29]

EAST ASIA

Country	Religious Affiliation
China	Buddhist 18.2%, Christian 5.1%, Muslim 1.8%, folk religion 21.9%, Hindu < .1%, Jewish < .1%, other 0.7% (includes Daoist (Taoist)), unaffiliated 52.2%. Note: officially atheist (2010 est.)
Hong Kong	Eclectic mixture of local religions 90%, Christian 10%
Japan	Shintoism 79.2%, Buddhism 66.8%, Christianity 1.5%, other 7.1%. Note: total adherents exceeds 100% because many practices both Shintoism and Buddhism (2012 est.)
Macau	Buddhist 50%, Roman Catholic 15%, none or other 35% (1997 est.)
Mongolia	Buddhist 53%, Muslim 3%, Christian 2.2%, Shamanist 2.9%, other 0.4%, none 38.6% (2010 est.)
North Korea	traditionally Buddhist and Confucianist, some Christian and syncretic Chondogyo (Religion of the Heavenly Way)
South Korea	Christian 31.6% (Protestant 24%, Roman Catholic 7.6%), Buddhist 24.2%, other or unknown 0.9%, none 43.3% (2010 survey)
Taiwan	Mixture of Buddhist and Taoist 93%, Christian 4.5%, other 2.5%

SOUTHEAST ASIA

Country	Religious Affiliation
Myanmar (Burma)	Buddhist 89%, Christian 4% (Baptist 3%, Roman Catholic 1%), Muslim 4%, Animist 1%, other 2%
Cambodia	Buddhist (official) 96.9%, Muslim 1.9%, Christian 0.4%, other 0.8% (2008 est.)
Indonesia	Muslim 87.2%, Christian 7%, Roman Catholic 2.9%, Hindu 1.7%, other 0.9% (includes Buddhist and Confucian), unspecified 0.4% (2010 est.)
Laos	Buddhist 66.8%, Christian 1.5%, other 31%, unspecified 0.7% (2005 est.)
Malaysia	Muslim (official) 61.3%, Buddhist 19.8%, Christian 9.2%, Hindu 6.3%, Confucianism, Taoism, other traditional Chinese religions 1.3%, other 0.4%, none 0.8%, unspecified 1% (2010 est.)
Philippines	Catholic 82.9%, Muslim 5%, Evangelical 2.8%, Iglesia ni Kristo 2.3%, other Christian 4.5%, other 1.8%, unspecified 0.6%, none 0.1% (2000 census)
Singapore	Buddhist 33.9%, Muslim 14.3%, Taoist 11.3%, Catholic 7.1%, Hindu 5.2%, other Christian 11%, other 0.7%, none 16.4% (2010 est.)
Thailand	Buddhist (official) 93.6%, Muslim 4.9%, Christian 1.2%, other 0.2%, none 0.1% (2010 est.)
Vietnam	Buddhist 9.3%, Catholic 6.7%, Hoa Hao 1.5%, Cao Dai 1.1%, Protestant 0.5%, Muslim 0.1%, none 80.8% (1999 census)

SOUTH ASIA

Country	Religious Affiliation
Afghanistan	Muslim 99.7% (Sunni 84.7–89.7%, Shia 10–15%), other 0.3% (2009 est.)
Bangladesh	Muslim 89.1%, Hindu 10%, other 0.9% (includes Buddhist, Christian) (2013 est.)
Bhutan	Lamaistic Buddhist 75.3%, Indian- and Nepalese-influenced Hinduism 22.1%, other 2.6% (2005 est.)
India	Hindu 79.8%, Muslim 14.2%, Christian 2.3%, Sikh 1.7%, other and unspecified 2% (2011 est.)
Maldives	Sunni Muslim (official)
Nepal	Hindu 81.3%, Buddhist 9%, Muslim 4.4%, Kirant 3.1%, Christian 1.4%, other 0.5%, unspecified 0.2% (2011 est.)
Pakistan	Muslim (official) 96.4% (Sunni 85–90%, Shia 10–15%), other (includes Christian and Hindu) 3.6% (2010 est.)
Sri Lanka	Buddhist (official) 70.2%, Hindu 12.6%, Muslim 9.7%, Roman Catholic 6.1%, other Christian 1.3%, other 0.05% (2012 est.)

As shown above, in most Asian countries, Christianity is a minority religion. It is a common perception that when the majority of people in a country profess faith in a particular religion that the country becomes closely associated with the religion. For example, Thailand is known as a Buddhist country.

In a similar way, America is commonly known as a Christian nation (or at least strongly influenced by Judeo-Christian values), though that perception is eroding as American society has become much more pluralistic with immigration from many parts of the world and more progressive in its social values.

Nevertheless, as millions of Asians have immigrated to America, their exposure and receptivity to Christianity is greatly increased because the United States is a majority Christian country. Compare and contrast the religious affiliation data in Asia with these in North America:

NORTH AMERICA

Country	Religious Affiliation
United States	Protestant 51.3%, Roman Catholic 23.9%, Mormon 1.7%, other Christian 1.6%, Jewish 1.7%, Buddhist 0.7%, Muslim 0.6%, other or unspecified 2.5%, unaffiliated 12.1%, none 4% (2007 est.)
Canada	Catholic 40.6% (includes Roman Catholic 38.8%, Orthodox 1.6%, other Catholic .2%), Protestant 20.3% (includes United Church 6.1%, Anglican 5%, Baptist 1.9%, Lutheran 1.5%, Pentecostal 1.5%, Presbyterian 1.4%, other Protestant 2.9%), other Christian 6.3%, Muslim 3.2%, Hindu 1.5%, Sikh 1.4%, Buddhist 1.1%, Jewish 1%, other 0.6%, none 23.9% (2011 est.)

CHRISTIANITY IN ASIA

To get an overview of the Gospel's receptivity in Asia, I aggregated the populations for the 3 regional groupings along with its percentage of Christians:

East Asians have a total population of 1,602,645,319 with 5.56% Christian, which is 89,088,497.

Southeast Asians have a total population of 634,446,116 with 20.54% Christian, which is 130,306,412 Christians.

South Asians have a total population of 1,707,043,483 with 1.84% Christian, which calculates to 31,369,548 Christians.

Looking at these numbers instead of just percentages is staggering. Did you know there are more Southeast Asians who are Christians than East Asians? (Note that this Christian population includes both Catholics and Protestants.) And the five Asian countries with the most Christians are: Philippines (91.1M), China (69.7M), India (28.8M), Indonesia (25.3M), and South Korea (15.5M).

It's encouraging to see that faithful followers of Christ have spread the Gospel throughout parts of Asia and the response in some Asian countries have resulted in millions of Christians. While I can't go into details on every country's history of how they were first introduced to the Gospel, I do encourage you to study the history of Christianity for the specific countries that you're most interested in.

Two countries with the largest proportion of Christians are the Philippines (90.2%) and South Korea (31.6%). The Philippines is proud to be "the only Christian nation in Asia," according to an Asia Society article, that goes on to describe the impact of Catholicism:

> The results of 400 years of Catholicism were mixed—ranging from a deep theological understanding by the educated elite to a more superficial understanding by the rural and urban masses. The latter is commonly referred to as Filipino folk Christianity, combining a surface veneer of Christian monotheism and dogma with indigenous animism.[30]

South Korean Christianity is noteworthy for its missionary zeal and its very large churches (5 of the world's largest churches are in South Korea).[31] This Christian heritage has also carried over by Korean immigrants into the United States: currently, Korean American churches are the most numerous amongst Asian American churches (more details in the next chapter).

This excerpt from *The Spirit Moves West: Korean Missionaries in America* by Rebecca Y. Kim summarizes the significance of Christianity for South Koreans:

> The impressive growth of Christianity is partly due to Koreans' response to drastic social transformation ... Koreans became identity-and community-seekers, and the Christian faith and community were there to fill the void. ... it mattered for the growth of the Korean Protestant church that the Protestant faith came to the Korean people at moments of tremendous crisis and change as a religion of modernity and power sans the heavy baggage of Western colonialism. ... On a per capita basis, South Korea sends out the most missionaries in the world. In 2011, there were approximately 20,000 Korean missionaries working in countries outside South Korea. ... A century after the advent of American missionary activity in Korea, South Korea has become a major missionary-sending nation.[32]

The third Asian country to pay attention to is China. The growth of Christianity in China is rapidly accelerating—estimated at 68 million in 2010 and projected to reach 160 million by 2025—and will make China the largest Christian nation in the world, according to Professor Fenggang Yang, author of *Religion in China: Survival and Revival under Communist Rule*.[33]

In the next chapter, we will take a closer look at the religious faiths of Asian Americans and how Asian American Christianity has taken shape in the U.S.

CHAPTER 3
OVERVIEW OF ASIAN AMERICAN CHRISTIANITY

We've already seen how diverse the Asian American demographic is ethnically and culturally; in a similar fashion, Asian Americans are very diverse religiously and spiritually as well. The religious affiliations of Asian Americans span a wide spectrum, as implied by the title of the Pew report, "Asian Americans: A *Mosaic of Faiths*"[34] (Italics my own). While there's much in the report about many other religions, this chapter takes a closer look at Asian American Christianity.

The Pew report cites that the overall survey shows 42% of Asian Americans self-identify as Christian, that is, 22% Protestant and 19% Catholic. (Note that these survey results also indicate that 75% of the U.S. general public self-identify as Christians.)

CHURCHED ASIAN AMERICANS

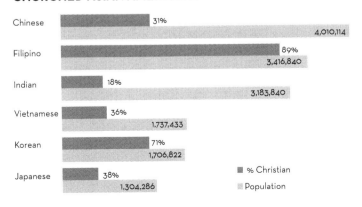

When you look at the numbers across ethnic lines, you'll notice something very different for each ethnic group. As the chart illustrates, the most churched are Filipino Americans and Korean Americans, with a majority of Filipino Americans being Catholic while a majority of Korean Americans being Protestant.

Furthermore, the Pew report compares and contrasts the receptivity of Christianity by an Asian ethnic group in America vs. the Asian country of origin:

> These proportions generally reflect the religious composition of each group's country of origin. The Philippines, for example, is heavily Catholic. In some cases, however, the percentage of Christians among Asian-American subgroups is much higher than in their ancestral lands. For example, 31% of the Chinese Americans surveyed are Christian; the vast majority, though not all, of this group come from mainland China, where Christians generally are estimated to constitute about 5% of the total population. Similarly, 18% of Indian Americans identify as Christian, though only about 3% of India's total population is estimated to be Christian. The higher percentages of Christians are a result of the disproportionate number of Christians who choose to migrate to the United States and may also reflect religious switching by immigrants.

Let's visualize these numbers as a side-by-side comparison of the Christian (both Protestant and Catholic) population in the Asian country of origin versus in the United States for the 6 largest Asian American ethnic groups:

COMPARISON OF CHRISTIAN POPULATION: ASIA VS. AMERICA

Country	% Christian in Country of Origin	% Christian in USA
China	5.1%	31%
Philippines	90.2%	89%
India	2.3%	18%
Vietnam	7.2%	36%
South Korea	31.6%	71%
Japan	1.5%	38%

Notice the phenomena that almost every Asian ethnic group has a much higher percentage of Christians in America than in their corresponding Asian country of origin. Why might this be? It could be attributed to being in a country where Christianity has had a stronger influence historically, along with the creative evangelistic methods developed in America's free market environment.

I've also heard this tendency is an indicator that Asians in America are more receptive to the Gospel. When people relocate to a new country, that disruption is a huge opportunity for changes in many areas, including one's spirituality and religious affiliation.

It should also be noted that most (if not all) Asian American churches are very intentional at providing practical ministries and services to the Asian immigrants. These good deeds open the hearts of immigrants to the Good News too.

What does all of this mean? A couple of caveats to keep in mind. First, there are distinctly unique narratives and timelines when each Asian ethnic group immigrated to the United States. This affects each group's rate of assimilation into the American culture, particularly for the next generations.

Second, these statistics are useful as a point of reference that shows a big picture of Asian American Christians like an impressionistic painting with broad paintbrushes. We can see the different Asian ethnicities' response to the Gospel and the difference between Asians in Asia versus Asians in America. However, these statistics are not to be used as a detailed road map or as a photograph to recognize individual faces. There are numerous differences for each Asian ethnicity just as there are many differences between individuals.

In other words, use these statistics to get some basic understanding about different Asian ethnicities, but don't overgeneralize or use these statistics against people by stereotyping. What we have learned here is a little bit more, definitely not everything, about each Asian American culture. To have some knowledge is better than ignorance.

As Asian American Christians come to faith, they also come together and organize into churches. These churches provide a tangible expression of their Christian faith that is particularly meaningful for them accordingly to their cultural value for group-oriented cohesion.

Through available research, here are the estimated numbers of ethnic Asian churches in the U.S.:[35]

ETHNIC ASIAN CHURCHES IN THE U.S.

Ethnicity	Estimated Count
Korean	4,653
Chinese	1,679
Asian Indian	1,317
Vietnamese	300
Filipino	200
Japanese	190
Hmong	171
Indonesian	124
Pakistani	120
Nepali	110
Cambodian	80
Lao	48
Thai	33
Bangladeshi	20
Sri Lankan	15
Burmese	15
Estimated Total	9,075

This estimate of 9,045 ethnic Asian American churches include over 4,600 Korean and over 1,600 Chinese churches. While exact numbers of Asian American churches are difficult to obtain, having estimates does provide some data for strategizing ministry. It is reasonable to say that a majority of these ethnic churches have worship services only in their respective Asian language, with a minority of them also having an English ministry, by necessity of ministering to the children of the immigrant families. (I've been exhorted by Asian pastors that one should use the term "ethnic Asian church," instead of "immigrant Asian church," when referring to a church that is primarily reaching first generation Asian Americans.)

Incidentally, these estimates for the total number of Protestant ethnic Asian churches don't quite add up. An average church is usually under 100 people in size; so 9,000 ethnic churches would mean around 900,000 people. That is far short of the 4 million people that supposedly make up 22% of Asian American Protestants as surveys have indicated.

This could imply a number of things: perhaps Asian Americans, like non-Asian Americans, default their religious affiliation to Christianity when responding to surveys in order to fit in. I'd say it's unlikely that so many Asian Americans are attending non-Asian or multi-ethnic churches. It also could be that thousands of ethnic Asian churches are unaccounted for, but I think that's less likely. There are also some Christians that belong to house churches that would not be counted with the formally-organized churches. While I could speculate and come up with more reasons to try to explain why these numbers don't fit together, I think it's better to recognize the limitation of surveys and statistics as a general point of reference for overall trends; they're not a reliably accurate means for measuring such an intangible thing as people's religious affiliations.

What this does say is: we need a lot more churches to reach this fastest-growing demographic of Asian Americans.

In the next chapter, we'll describe the common models of Asian American churches and how church governance is structured and organized for effective ministry.

CHAPTER 4

ASIAN AMERICAN CHURCH MODELS

Whether Asian Americans brought their Christian faith with them as immigrants or they became Christians while residing in the United States, the natural outcome is the formation of churches and worshipping communities.

Over the years, Asian American churches have developed using a variety of models to navigate the different languages and cultures of multiple Asian American generations. As a part of this process, church leaders organized around the uniqueness of each generation. The first generation refers to people who are foreign-born, speaks the corresponding Asian language most fluently while the second generation refers to those who are American-born with English as their primary language.

Also note that several Asian ethnicities have coined their own terms to identify themselves. For Chinese Americans, the first generation is known as "OBC," an acronym for Overseas-Born Chinese. The second generation is known as "ABC," which stands for American-Born Chinese. And the acronym "ARC" means American-Raised Chinese, someone who was foreign-born and immigrated to the U.S. under the age of 18. In the Korean American context, "1.0" refers to the first generation, "2.0" refers to the second generation, and "1.5" refers to someone foreign-born and immigrated under the age of 18. Japanese Americans may use the terms Issei, Nisei, and Sansei to refer to the first, second, and third generation.

Biologically and mathematically speaking, the second generation are the children of first generation immigrants. This implies that the strong Asian cultural value for social structure through the hierarchy of a parent-child relationship will greatly influence and be taken into consideration by pastors and church leaders working in Asian American churches.

Christian leaders have observed and described the variety of Asian American church models in three different ways. Let me introduce them to you as general points of reference.

CHURCH MODELS AS RELATIONSHIPS

First, Asian American church models may be described based on relationships. These are based on articles by Pastor Ken Carlson and Rev. Victor Lee as they've observed how Chinese churches in North America often go through three stages:[36]

1. Paternal (Father/Son) Model
Asian churches typically start with a leadership structure that basically follows the Asian culture, with the first generation leaders running the church in the same way they run the family. As children are born and grow up, there's a natural progression for starting a nursery, a children's ministry, and later on, a youth ministry. Since these children grow up speaking English in America, ministry is provided in English. These ministries are typically viewed as a part of the church's Christian education program. This type of church would prioritize having a worship service exclusively in the corresponding Asian language. When English-speaking adults start coming to the church, either from outreach or from biology, the church temporarily accommodates this for a short time with a worship service that has both Asian and English languages through translation.

2. Parallel Model
As more English-speaking adults become part of the church, ministries will be led by English-speaking leaders. Gradually over time, this may include a separate English worship service, separate English fellowships, and other ministries that run in parallel with

the Asian-language ministries. These separate ministries allow each language group to have some autonomy to customize their ministries to be more effective. However, the church's leadership structure remains predominantly held by first generation leaders who make decisions affecting the whole church.

3. Partnership Model

In this model, the church leadership structure and governing policy is changed to empower both language ministries as interdependent partners. Each language ministry would have its own board or council to oversee its ministries, with a joint formed for policies or issues that affect the whole church.

CHURCH MODELS AS RESIDENCES

Second, Asian American church models may be described as types of residences with housing metaphors. I heard these described in a class lecture by Dr. Benjamin Shin (Talbot School of Theology at Biola University) in the Asian American ministry track of the Doctor of Ministry program. These models will be fully detailed in Dr. Shin's book titled, *Tapestry of Grace: Untangling the Cultural Complexities in Asian American Life and Ministry*, co-authored with Dr. Sheryl Takagi Silzer. I will provide a general overview of these models.[37] You'll notice that these models describe both specifically Asian American churches as well as non-Asian churches where Asian Americans attend.

1. "Room for Rent" Model

This model describes a church started and led by first generation Asian Americans. To accommodate their children, corresponding English ministries to children and youth would be started over time, typically in a room of the church, and thus the name for this model.

2. "Duplex" Model

This model has two congregations side-by-side: the Asian-language congregation and the English-language congregation. One church with two congregations is like a duplex house with two units under one roof, that is, under one leadership which primarily or completely consists of first generation Asian-language church leaders. This model would evolve from the "Room for Rent" model to accommodate a English worship service.

3. "Triplex" Model

This model describes a Chinese American church that has three language congregations: Mandarin, Cantonese, and English. Three congregations, each with a worship service in their own language/dialect, live together under a single church leadership.

4. "Townhouse" Model

This model describes two language congregations with two separate leaderships but share one church facility, whether that's one building or one campus. You could call this: "two churches, one location." Separate leadership here means there are separate constitutions, with decision-making autonomy and independent budgets. Yet, these two organizations have agreed to do ministry together across multiple generations and cultures.

5. "Hotel" Model

These are English-speaking Asian Americans who attend a very large church, typically a megachurch (defined as churches with weekend attendance over 2,000 adults and children). These majority-culture churches reach a wide range of demographics through a larger number of professionally-produced programs and ministries that can result in a personalized individual experience, similar to having a private room in a hotel.

6. "Satellite" Model

This model describes one church in multiple locations, also known as a "multi-site" church.[38] Churches are extending their ministry to more people in multiple locations by using this model. A significant percentage of these churches will use video to deliver its sermon from a teaching pastor to the worship services at satellite locations. Only a small percentage of these churches actually use live satellite feeds, since there are more affordable alternative technologies available today.

7. "2 for 1" Model

This model is two language congregations led by one bilingual pastor, who is fluent in both languages and able to lead both first and second generations. The requirements and responsibilities of a pastor leading this type of church is uniquely demanding, but it can work with someone who is in that "1.5" or "ARC" generation.

8. "Church Plant" Model

This model is not just describing any church that's been planted as a startup church, like an ethnic Asian church plant or a non-Asian church plant. In the context of this book, this model is describing a new church that's been planted by a second generation Asian American pastor who is reaching a significant number of Asian Americans beyond what the original (mother) church could by itself. Many of these church plants reach beyond one particular English-speaking Asian American ethnicity and intentionally reach other Asian Americans as well as non-Asians too. There's much more to be said about this model—and that's what will be unpacked in the following chapters.

MANY CHURCH MODELS

Helen Lee, author of the 1996 article titled, "Silent Exodus,"[39] (arguably the first significant and widely-circulated article describing the trend of English-speaking Asian Americans leaving their ethnic Asian churches) writes about 6 types of Asian American church models in this 2014 article—this is an abbreviated summary:[40]

1. The Asian Immigrant Church

Asian American immigrants (first generation) started these churches primarily to reach other immigrants of the same ethnicity. These churches would have ministries to their English-speaking children and youth while retaining its strong ethnic identity.

2. The English-Ministry Offshoot

English-speaking adults in the second generation (and subsequent generations) take ownership for their church ministries while remaining closely connected to the Asian immigrant congregation. In some cases they even launch fully-independent churches.

3. The Historic Church
Some Asian immigrant churches were started over a century ago by Japanese Americans or Chinese Americans. Some have evolved into pan-Asian or multi-ethnic churches, while others hold on to their cultural heritage. A few even do both.

4. The Pan-Asian American Church
Some Asian American churches have a primary focus on reaching English-speaking Asian Americans from multiple Asian ethnicities. This includes churches that have launched with an intentional focus, as well as those that have transitioned over time from an Asian immigrant church.

5. The Multiethnic Church
Some Asian American pastors have launched new churches with the goal to reach diverse multiethnic and multiracial demographics- a mixture of Asians and non-Asians alike, and at times including socio-economic diversity.

6. The House Church
Some Asian Americans are forming missional church expressions in smaller gatherings that don't require a church building or public venue.

Now that we've looked at a number of different ways to describe Asian American church models, the underlying question that drives all of these different models is: **How will the church reach English-speaking Asian Americans?**

All kinds of issues arise in a church that's bringing together Asian Americans from multiple generations due to differences in language, cultural values, leadership styles and structures, worship preferences, etc. A number of books and many more dissertations have done extensive research to try to explain these issues. (A brief list and more titles can be found in the bibliography and at multiasian.church.) Here is a common theme I found in these books and writings: There are too many layers of complexities and no easy answers. It should be noted too, that these ministry challenges are not exclusive to Asian Americans; other racial and ethnic groups are dealing with their own difficulties serving multi-generational congregations too.

CHOOSING THE RIGHT CHURCH MODEL

When I talk with first generation Asian church leaders, I'm frequently asked this question: "What's the best model for an ethnic Asian church?" or "What's the right model?" My answer is usually that there isn't only one way to do ministry effectively. I believe the Bible gives us a lot of freedom for discerning how to organize and structure a church's leadership and ministries.

Look at the many Christian denominations and sects. Some believe that a congregational form of church government is best, while others believe in a church polity such as Presbyterian, Episcopalian, Methodist, Lutheran, Baptist, or thousands of others. There is a wide variety in how churches may govern itself, but we all worship the same Triune God, put our faith in the same Bible while upholding orthodoxy.

Those of us that are called to be church leaders are entrusted with an important stewardship. Part of that role of leading is to discern and decide what is the best model to use for our particular context and time.

And that's the hard work of leading a church: deciding on which model to use for effective ministry now, and discerning when it's time to change to a different church model. To quote something I've learned from Leadership Network: no model is perfect; some are helpful.

In other publications I've seen, authors often present church models with a list of pros and cons, advantages and disadvantages.

What I think may be more helpful is for me to share some brief guidance on when each church model can be the most effective, using Dr. Benjamin Shin's list of church models:

- "Room for Rent" model is perhaps most practical for a normal-sized church of under 120 in attendance.
- "Duplex" model is useful for providing language-specific worship services separately in order to minister to each generation in its own first language for basic spiritual growth.
- "Triplex" model is useful for worship services and ministries for three language groups.
- "Townhouse" model can be more effective for developing leadership in both languages and both generations in order to increase outreach and discipleship.
- "Hotel" models are great at providing high-quality ministries to a wider range of demographics.
- "Satellite" models are good for bringing highly-effective church ministries to multiple locations.
- "2 for 1" model can work if the pastor has the right profile and gift mix
- "Church Plant" model is extremely challenging but has a greater potential at reaching non-Christians through evangelism (since outreach is essential for its survival).

WHEN TO SWITCH CHURCH MODELS

The harder work of church leadership is discerning when it's time to change to a different church model. And, it's wiser to discern beforehand when your church needs to change before it's too late. Your church doesn't have to wait until everything is falling apart before making changes.

Exodus 18:13-26 tells the story of how Moses waited a little too long to make the change before being overworked. His father-in-law eventually advised him to delegate the work to others:

> The next day Moses sat to judge the people, and the people stood around Moses from morning till evening. When Moses' father-in-law saw all that he was doing for the people, he said, "What is

this that you are doing for the people? Why do you sit alone, and all the people stand around you from morning till evening?" And Moses said to his father-in-law, "Because the people come to me to inquire of God; when they have a dispute, they come to me and I decide between one person and another, and I make them know the statutes of God and his laws." Moses' father-in-law said to him, "What you are doing is not good. You and the people with you will certainly wear yourselves out, for the thing is too heavy for you. You are not able to do it alone. Now obey my voice; I will give you advice, and God be with you! You shall represent the people before God and bring their cases to God, and you shall warn them about the statutes and the laws, and make them know the way in which they must walk and what they must do. Moreover, look for able men from all the people, men who fear God, who are trustworthy and hate a bribe, and place such men over the people as chiefs of thousands, of hundreds, of fifties, and of tens. And let them judge the people at all times. Every great matter they shall bring to you, but any small matter they shall decide themselves. So it will be easier for you, and they will bear the burden with you. If you do this, God will direct you, you will be able to endure, and all this people also will go to their place in peace."

So Moses listened to the voice of his father-in-law and did all that he had said. Moses chose able men out of all Israel and made them heads over the people, chiefs of thousands, of hundreds, of fifties, and of tens. And they judged the people at all times. Any hard case they brought to Moses, but any small matter they decided themselves.

It was a good thing that Moses took his father-in-law's advice and appointed others to share the work of governing people. In other words, Moses restructured his organization.

Similarly, there's a time when churches need to switch to a new church model. There are stages in the life of a church when restructuring and reorganizing the model of ministry is necessary.

In an Asian American context, this has particular challenges. One challenge comes from Asian cultures having longer histories of many centuries in comparison to the United States' 200 plus years of history. Consequently, Asians tend to change more slowly than Americans, and older people change slower than younger people. There is also an Asian cultural value for traditions and memories, in contrast to American culture's value for innovation and novelty.

To be fair, most people don't like change. Both Asian Americans and other Americans have resistance to change. Change is stressful because it introduces the fear of uncertainty and triggers anxiety about the unknown. Life is much easier and more comfortable when things are known and predictably routine.

With this in mind, that change is difficult for a majority of people, and church leaders must carefully consider God's Word and be in prayer when discerning the times for change. And, we should be careful not to over-spiritualize. Making organizational change has to be guided by spiritually mature leadership but also implemented practically and skillfully over time. For the spiritual part, I'll point you to God and His Word.

To summarize, let me reiterate how challenging and complicated organizational changes can be. There's a whole field of study with degrees being offered by universities on change management in organizational life.

This is not to say that you have to have a degree in organizational management to be effective in leading change in your church. But you will have to prepare your church's leadership when taking on these challenges. And it may be valuable to get help from denominational resources or church consulting groups.

3 resources I'd suggest as starting points for your church leadership to learn more about the process of guiding your congregation through change are:

Before You Lead Your Church Through Change by Pastor Rick Warren
8 Step Biblical Process for Leading Change based on Acts 15
Leading Change without Losing It by Carey Nieuwhof

CHAPTER 5
NEXT GENERATION MULTI-ASIAN CHURCHES

You've probably heard the saying, "We've never done it that way before." Here's the thing: if we keep on doing the same things that we've been doing but expect different results, that's just not going to happen. You have to do things differently to get different results.

My first job after pastoring was working part-time at a family foundation. L² Foundation is a private foundation founded by Paul and Alice Chou, with a mission to develop the leadership and legacy of Asian Americans for Kingdom impact. The Chous have been blessed by the generosity of God and wanted to be a blessing to others. For ten years, I was a part of facilitating opportunities and gathering resources to catalyze next generation Asian American leaders. Highlights include these two books published by L² Foundation: *Asian American Youth Ministry* and *Conversations: Asian American Evangelical Theologies in Formation.*[41]

From 2006 to 2009, I worked as a program director through a partnership formed between L² Foundation and Leadership Network. Leadership Network has a mission to work with innovative church leaders to multiply their impact in ministry. I got to be a part of developing what that would look like in an Asian American context. In other words, I was on point to identify the innovations among Asian American churches.

What I have discovered is that there are growing numbers of new churches reaching the next generation of Asian Americans. Here's a picture showing this numerical growth over the past 15 years:

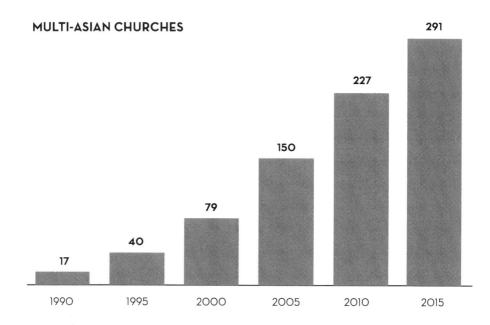

MULTI-ASIAN CHURCHES

17	40	79	150	227	291
1990	1995	2000	2005	2010	2015

DIGGING INTO THE DEFINITION

The phrase "next generation multi-Asian" is a portmanteau. "Next generation" refers to the multiple generations of Asian Americans who are American-born, chronologically speaking, including the second generation (or "2.0" in Korean American circles), third generation, even fourth or fifth generation. This term also encompasses Asian Americans who are biracial, those who are children of parents with different ethnicities, whether that's two different Asian ethnicities (e.g. Korean married to Chinese) or someone with one Asian parent and one non-Asian parent (e.g. Caucasian, African American, or Latino American). When I talk with pastors who lead these next generation multi-Asian churches, I have found that a vast majority of these churches do not self-identify as Asian American churches, even though many of their congregations consist of over 80% Asian Americans. And to be fair, none of them would identify as being a multi-Asian church either. There are reasons for this non-identification: for one, the church may have a vision to just be a church without drawing any attention to its demographics. This thinking often comes from a theological premise that the Gospel of Jesus Christ is for all peoples (citing Bible passages Galatians 3:28 or Revelation 7:9), and the church should be welcoming people of all ethnic backgrounds.

Other churches will explicitly identify themselves as being a multi-ethnic church, in order to express the intentionality to work at being diverse ethnically, racially, and for some, socio-economically.

There are other ways to describe "multi-Asian." In sociological circles, other terms used to describe this demographic include pan-Asian, Asian-American, Asian Pacific Americans (APA), or Asian American and Native Hawaiian Pacific Islanders (NHPI). These terms don't adequately describe the multiple Asian ethnic groups coming together in an English-speaking church. In fact, "pan-Asian churches" is a term that's currently used by some scholars and experts. I found these terms lacking because they should be inclusive of the non-Asians that were part of these churches and acknowledge the aspirations of these pastors towards becoming multiethnic churches.

"Third culture" is a term used for Asian Americans with bicultural background. The term originated from "third culture kid (TCK)," which was first coined by researchers John and Ruth Useem in the 1950s. They used it to describe the children of American citizens working and living abroad. These are children who were raised in a culture outside of their parents' culture for a significant part of their developmental years. The TCK experience is unique in that these individuals moved between cultures before fully developing their personal and cultural identity. While "third culture" describes well the fluidity of a multi-cultural, multi-ethnic, and multi-racial context that multi-Asian churches cultivate, it does not acknowledge the Asian American contribution to these multi-ethnic churches. Commonly used terms like "third culture" and "multi-ethnic" does not capture the importance of Asian Americans in these kinds of churches.

This new wave of churches is a new thing which should be called out with a new term. In my conversation with pastors of multi-Asian churches, they seem to accept the term "multi-Asian." They preferred this descriptive term more than "Asian American."

The final reason is that next generation multi-Asian churches would be considered as using a "church plant" model, very different from an English ministry existing within an ethnic Asian church, like those in a Duplex, Triplex, or Townhouse models (see Chapter 4: Asian American Church Models). The word "churches" in the term "next generation multi-Asian churches" is precisely intended to note the autonomy and independence of these churches that are led and governed from an ethnic Asian church. When a church has its own governance, with its own finances and its own constitution, it bears all of its own responsibilities and begins to shape its own distinct identity.

It should be noted that not all church plants by Asian Americans are next generation multi-Asian churches. There are also a growing number of Asian-language churches being planted to reach first generation Asian immigrants. In my own informal research, the estimated number of Asian American churches has grown 27%: From 7,123 in 2007[42] to 9,075 in 2016.[43] From a 2014 report, 1,787 Asian congregations are in the Southern Baptist Convention, up 54.3% from 1998 to 2013.[44]

RESEARCH FINDINGS

Going back to my story from the beginning of this chapter, during my time at L² Foundation and Leadership Network, I started my research by contacting Asian American churches and pastors, both informally through interviews and formally through a survey. The survey results were published in the 2007 report, "Asian American Churches: An Introductory Survey."[45] Here are three highlights from this report:

- Asian American churches are diversifying ethnically–
  79% have at least 10% non-Asians in attendance

- Active church planting to reach more people—61% are planning to launch new churches
- Missionary zeal is evident—61% send out career missionaries

I also started compiling a list of Asian American church plants. I worked with the assumption that what we have in common as Asian American churches, amidst all of its diversity with cultures, languages, and generations, is Jesus Christ, the Bible, and the English language, albeit to varying degrees.

Additionally, through that joint partnership between L² Foundation and Leadership Network, we hosted a handful of gatherings with next generation Asian American pastors to connect leaders with one another. One of the principles behind these gatherings is found in Proverbs 27:17: "Iron sharpens iron, and one man sharpens another." We brought these pastors together to sharpen one another through a process that facilitates result-based conversations.

The list of Asian American church continues to grow in numbers, perhaps even exponentially. Time will tell. Initially, I had maintained the list through a wiki platform called Wetpaint. By 2012, with over 200 churches, I migrated the list into an online spreadsheet to better manage this growing list.[46] With that move, I coined the phrase "Next Generation Multi-Asian Churches" to describe this growing phenomena.

Working with innovative church leaders at Leadership Network really energized me. I discovered that I had a knack for keeping an eye out for the new things that God is doing in and through His people. This definition of innovation was adapted from Peter Drucker: "Innovation is change that creates a new level of performance."[47]

In the following chapters, we'll take a closer look at the characteristics and traits, including real-life stories of these next generation multi-Asian churches.

CHAPTER 6
CHARACTERISTICS AND TRAITS

The most frequently asked question about next generation multi-Asian churches, after its definition, is its characteristics and traits. What are the characteristics and traits of these churches and how do they differ from the typical ethnic Asian church? What do they look like?

Before I describe the common characteristics, note that there's a wide variety of Asian American churches because of the wide diversity of many Asian ethnicities, languages, and cultures. It should be obvious that a Chinese person going to a Korean church or Vietnamese church would probably feel just as lost going to a Caucasian church. The experience of the Christian life is more than language alone; it also involves culture, relationships, and theology. In the new book by Dr. Benjamin Shin and Dr. Sheryl Takagi Silzer, *Tapestry of Grace: Untangling the Cultural Complexities in Asian American Life and Ministry*, there is a chapter that presents a comparison of Chinese and Korean spirituality on how their cultural perspectives affect various aspects of their Christianity, including spiritual habits, faith expressions, and view of pastors.

Let me first recognize the similarities that most, if not all, Asian American churches have, both the ones that are reaching first generation foreign-born immigrants and their American-born subsequent generations:

Marginalization – Asian Americans have a shared experience as a minority racial group in an American society with a majority that's largely Caucasian, followed by Latino and African Americans. American history has been blemished with injustices that discriminated against Asians in America, including the Chinese Exclusion Act of 1882, Japanese internment camps, as well as portraying racially insensitive and offensive Asian stereotypes in television and movies. The reality of being Asian American in an imperfect American society is that having an Asian face will be the subject of unjust discrimination, prejudices, misunderstandings, and unintentional offenses.

Group-oriented – Growing up around Asians cultivates the deferential habit of thinking first about the group's collective needs over one's individual preferences. Here's an example: this socialization may be observed on the occasion of a small group having a lengthy discussion deciding on where to eat for lunch.

Shame-based – Many Asian Americans have been affected by the honor-shame values of Asian cultures through their family history. This affects both their sense of belonging and how relationships are restored. Through her TED talks, books, and seminars, Brené Brown raises awareness of shame in American society (but I have to say that I don't think she adequately explains the nuances of shame in an Asian context). She aptly describes the difference between guilt and shame: guilt is, "I did something bad." Shame is, "I am bad." Guilt would say: "I'm sorry. I made a mistake." Shame would feel: "I'm sorry. I am a mistake."[48] In recent years, theologians like Jackson Wu (author of *Saving God's Face: A Chinese Contextualization of Salvation through Honor and Shame*) and Jayson Georges have articulated valuable insights about the Christian life and the Bible which better contextualize the honor-shame cultures.

Identify with a specific Asian ethnicity – Most Asian Americans self-identify with their ethnic heritage, rather than as a generic Asian American. (Note there may be an exception for children of mixed Asian parents, as in Korean married to Chinese, to self-identify as Asian American.) Typically, a next generation multi-Asian church will have a lineage traced to a specific Asian ethnicity, since it was likely planted by one. Even when that connection is not explicitly stated, a Vietnamese-American, for example, will intuitively and subconsciously recognize differences between one church with Korean-American lineage versus another church with Japanese-American lineage. In other words, having an English-speaking church doesn't mean that all Asian Americans from different ethnic backgrounds will easily come together.

Missions-mindedness – Ethnic Asian churches reaching first generation Asian immigrants have a natural affinity to bring the Gospel to people in their country of origin and other countries around the world because of their common language and ethnicity. Next generation multi-Asian churches tend to be strongly missions-minded, but often with a people group different from themselves. I've observed that while every church plant has to be actively evangelistic in its own community for its own survival and sustainability, it seems that next generation multi-Asian churches actively start participating in world missions in its early years.

Aside from the similarities, there are characteristics in these next generation multi-Asian churches that are different than ethnic Asian churches. While not every next generation multi-Asian church has all of these characteristics, these are the ones from most of the churches I have observed. Incidentally, there may be ethnic Asian churches reaching first generation immigrants that possess one (or more) of these characteristics. Obviously, the one characteristic that is common for all next generation multi-Asian churches is English-speaking.[49]

Here are five characteristics common with next generation multi-Asian churches, by corollary, less common with ethnic Asian churches.

LEADERSHIP

Next generation Asian Americans have grown up in an American context with a particular value for leadership development. The proliferation of many courses, books, and conferences on Christian leadership has become a prominent part of churches since the 1980s. It is partly due to our growing understanding in organizational management that is being applied in some churches to more effectively and efficiently fulfill its mission and vision. It's more acceptable among next generation multi-Asian churches to use vocabulary associated with strategic planning: mission, vision, values, strategies, tactics, results, and metrics. This is just how things are done in an American context. There isn't enough space to compare and contrast, but suffice it to say that American leadership styles are very different from Asian leadership styles.

Church leaders are identified and selected based on character and Christian maturity, according to 1 Timothy 3:1-7. For next generation Asian American church leaders, it is also based on competencies and alignment to vision, in contrast to a traditional Asian church's value for social status, age, and wealth. One next generation Asian American pastor, who has ministered in both cultural contexts, keenly observed this: "The priority leadership value in an American church is vision, while the priority value in an Asian church is family." I think that's a good summary.

To share with you one example of visionary leadership, let me share the one I know well. Pastor Ray Chang is the founding pastor of Ambassador Bible Church in Northern Virginia. We met while we were both at Dallas Theological Seminary in 1991. Even though he grew up in a typical immigrant Korean family, he didn't readily fit into a traditional ethnic Korean church. Ray's ministry background was greatly influenced through Christian ministries like Calvary Chapel, Evangelical Free Church of Fullerton, Biola University, and Talbot School of Theology.

A couple years later, Pastor Ray was pastoring a young English ministry at an ethnic Korean church (in a "townhouse" model, as described in Chapter 4). One day in a side conversation with one of his members, he asked the question, "Why don't you invite your non-Asian co-workers to our church?" The member reluctantly replied, "But this is a Korean-American church and they would feel uncomfortable." Pastor Ray began to see how easily a culture becomes the main reason for gathering, rather than Christ or His mission. While driving through Washington DC, Pastor Ray noticed the many embassies representing countries from all around the world; the verse from 2 Corinthians 5:20 came to mind: "We are therefore Christ's ambassadors, as though God were making his appeal through us. We implore you on Christ's behalf: Be reconciled to God."

Pastor Ray caught a vision for how the church could be an embassy for the Kingdom of God. With a dozen people in his apartment, God brought together this small multi-ethnic group to launch Ambassador Bible Church in 1996 with a multi-ethnic vision. This group of 12 had a kind of next generation multi-Asian diversity, with Korean Americans, Chinese Americans, and Caucasians in the mix.

I was invited to join Pastor Ray at Ambassador Bible Church as an associate pastor in Fall 1997 and we saw it grow from 70 to 140 in about 3 years. We saw people come to Christ from different nationalities and ethnicities. We saw how God provided through His people for His vision, and we met and exceeded our church budget every year. I still remember to this day the church's vision statement that we had to memorize in membership class: "To make and equip disciples from all nationalities to be Christ's ambassadors to all the nations."

Pastor Ray's visionary leadership laid a solid foundation for this church that has continued to this day. Ambassador Bible Church is now ever more diverse than ever, reaching over 400 in attendance, and reproducing by planting another multiethnic church just as this chapter is being written.

CREATIVITY

Many next generation multi-Asian churches have a value for creativity that's shown in its visual arts and presentation. When you visit their church websites, you'll see a contemporary web design with introductory information to welcome visitors and social media links along with recent sermons and church announcements. During a worship service, creativity may be seen in the use of video clips for sermon illustrations, energetic special music, or aesthetically-pleasing decoration in the worship and fellowship spaces. In contrast, an ethnic Asian church would more likely have formal traditions of hymns and a choir, invocation, or silent meditation.

Ekko Church embodies creative use of media to communicate the Gospel message in compellingly relevant ways that reaches next generation young adults, also known as the millennial generation.

During my first visit to Ekko Church in Fullerton, California, I found myself driving into an industrial area with warehouses near the local municipal airport. They met in a non-descript warehouse building with contemporary wood paneling on the outside. I recognized the church logo as I walked in, and was kindly greeted by a couple of young adults without being handed a church bulletin.

I walked into the worship space, which was dimly lit creating a quiet mood while soft music played in the background and a video loop of imagery played on the two rear-projection screens up front. It felt like a safe and inviting space. Wood paneling similar in style to what was outside engulfed the stage, where the drums, electric guitar, and electronic keyboard were set up for the worship band. A wooden cross stood at center stage.

The worship team came on stage, a word of welcome and opening prayer kicked off a time of worship that lasted about 45 minutes. Then there was a time of fellowship for a few minutes to chat and greet your neighbors. I estimate over 200 young adults filled the worship space that day. The sermon was shared in a conversational tone with good storytelling intermixed. I noticed an interesting juxtaposition—the band played behind the cross while the preacher delivered the sermon in front of it.

Ekko Church showed a lot of attention to detail in its visual and graphic design throughout—from the church website to the worship space. I found out later that the warehouse space is borrowed, and I think it's great that two churches would share space together to maximize its usage.

Ekko also published a beautifully-designed printed magazine to tell its stories and values in an engaging manner. A graphically-designed banner image complements every sermon series. Furthermore, their social media presence on Facebook and YouTube further extends its storytelling of doing life in community. As communications professor Marshall McLuhan's adage says, "the medium is the message."

SOCIAL JUSTICE

Many next generation multi-Asian churches recognize the value for all peoples beyond their own ethnicity. The Gospel of Jesus Christ is good news for the here and now, not only for eternal life in Heaven. In John 10:10, Jesus said: "I came that they may have life and have it abundantly." More specifically to social justice, the Bible says in Micah 6:8 (ESV), "He has told you, O man, what is good; and what does the Lord require of you but to do justice, and to love kindness, and to walk humbly with your God?" and in Isaiah 1:17 (ESV), "Learn to do good; seek justice, correct oppression; bring justice to the fatherless, plead the widow's cause."

In our world that is obviously broken with recent news of terrifying incidents of violence in America and elsewhere, the church has an urgent opportunity to take a more active role in bringing hope and healing to the whole world. Even here in America, one of the wealthiest of first-world nations, there is brokenness in our own backyard, and next generation multi-Asian churches want to be actively involved in serving their neighboring community. While an ethnic Asian church does well in serving immigrants of their own ethnicity, next generation churches are desiring to serve those in need within their immediate locality regardless of ethnicity or race.

The first example is a church with justice as one of its core values. Epic Church originated as an idea for a church that would reach a different kind of individuals who are not interested in the "normal" church. Founding pastor Kevin Doi, a next generation Asian American of Japanese descent, didn't grow up in a church. When he became a Christian, he had a difficult time finding a church that was a safe place for his friends, where hard questions could be asked, while ambiguity (not certainty) was embraced and appreciated. He also had a concern for healing and justice, wanting to help create a therapeutic community which addressed people's relational worlds and the systemic inequalities in society.

They started in 1998, with a small group of twenty-somethings meeting together in Orange County, California. They moved several times over the years, finally landing in Fullerton. In a major shift in ecclesiology and mission, Epic came to recognize that God had called them not to reach a certain group of individuals, but to commit themselves to a specific place.

One of the results of their new mission was the launching of JOYA Scholars, a non-profit organization inspiring and preparing students from underserved communities in Fullerton toward higher education. Now in its seventh year, JOYA Scholars is supported by civic and business leaders, school districts, and local colleges as well as universities. JOYA provides one-on-one mentoring, tutoring, college prep workshops and tours, with volunteers coming from Epic Church, Cal State Fullerton, other nearby churches, and the wider community.

The second example is a church that recognizes doing justice is an integral part of being faithful to living out the Gospel. Jeya and Daniel So make up the husband-and-wife team who planted Anchor City Church in San Diego at the start of 2014. Just like any church planting journey, discerning and responding to God's call to plant involved the convergence of many different factors. As 2.0 Korean Americans, both Jeya and Daniel understood what it meant to be outsiders—neither accepted as fully "American" because of their Asian faces, nor accepted as fully "Korean" either in Korea or in America. After serving in English ministries of ethnic Korean churches for many years, they began to sense a broader call to bless, serve, and reach the city—in all its fullness and diversity.

Drawing on their own experience of how God redeemed their sense of being "neither/nor" to become "both/and" people, Jeya and Daniel responded to God's call to plant a church where people who felt like outsiders, who could not find their place, or felt like they had one foot in two different worlds could experience deep friendship and community. Psalm 68:6, "God sets the lonely in families," has been a core guiding verse for Anchor City.

When I asked Pastor Daniel what makes Anchor City unique, he answered with a smile, "We're just a normal church." He went on further to explain that as pastors, the goal for he and Jeya is to awaken and empower each members of the church to live out their God-given dreams and on mission for Jesus—both in the context of serving at church as well as in the day to day—at the places they live, work, and play. Family and "the table" are guiding metaphors for Anchor City as they seek to build a faithful and fruitful community. Jeya and Daniel often joke with their church, "When we share meals together we open our mouths to the meal and our hearts to each other." At each Home Group meeting, they share not only Bible study and prayer requests, but a meal around a table.

In the two and half years since they planted, Anchor City has grown in attendance, but the numerical growth has tended to be slow and steady—some people have found the church through their website and social media presence, but the vast majority have come through word-of-mouth and relational connections. Because San Diego is a transitional city in many ways (difficult for young adults to find jobs), Anchor City has seen a number of people leave the area due to their work. They try to be intentional as a sending church, blessing people as they leave San Diego.

In pursuing whole-life discipleship, Anchor City has expressed their commitment to join in God's mission of redemption in the world both in words and in action. The pastors preach regularly on the importance of stewarding whole lives for God's glory and the importance of personal, relational evangelism. The church community has taken special Easter and Advent offerings where 100% of the giving went to nonprofit organizations serving foster care children, restoring victims of human trafficking in San Diego, and fighting modern-day slavery in India. Home Groups have prepared care packages for senior citizens, the youth group has partnered with local food banks, and Anchor City sent a vision team to Nepal last year—to learn from local pastors and leaders, and to partner with them in their faithful work.

CELEBRATORY WORSHIP

The music portion during a next generation multi-Asian church worship service is celebratory and contemporary, rather than solemn and reverent. The musical accompaniment is likely a five-piece band with drums, bass, keyboard, electric guitar, and acoustic guitar. The songs are mostly from the praise and worship genre, with popular songs by Passion, Bethel and Hillsong, with the likes of Chris Tomlin, Matt Redman, Kari Jobe, or Joel Houston.

In many ways, the sound of worship is similar to a corresponding evangelical church that is largely Caucasian in its majority. When you open your eyes and look around, however, those in attendance will appear far more ethnically diverse in the next generation multi-Asian church.

And the other differences are far more nuanced, noticeable only to the trained eyes and ears in the style of music played and how the songs are sung. And there are subtle differences between these next generation churches too. For churches with Chinese-American or Japanese-American roots, the worship music may be softer, slower, and more meditative. For churches with Korean-American roots, the worship music will be comparatively louder and sung expressively and more passionately. I've measured the loudness on an occasion and it was right up to 99 decibels in one Korean-American church.

AESTHETIC QUALITY

Partly due to valuing frugality, many ethnic Asian churches, combined with the immigration story of survival, perceive dispensing resources for art and aesthetics in a church setting as being a "waste of money." On the contrary, chances are you will not see a Xeroxed church bulletin at a next generation multi-Asian church.

For the next generation Asian American pastors, an American value for excellence in aesthetics is more visibly seen in its logo design, worship space decor, lighting, audio and visuals all embedded into everything that a church does. This isn't to say that the level of quality and production value in a next generation multi-Asian church could rival the high production value of a worship experience in a megachurch setting. But it is to say that there's an apparent difference between a next generation church versus the ethnic Asian church. It just looks and feels differently. Being married to an artist, I've received personal tutoring in the area of art appreciation.

To get a sense of what this characteristic looks like, you can browse the websites of next generation multi-Asian churches which are listed at multiasian.church/directory. To highlight a few, take a look at Quest Church, Church of the Beloved, and Vision Church.

ONE MORE THING

There are other characteristics that take on a certain flavor in next generation multi-Asian churches. Since everything is done in English, things look very similar to a typical mainstream evangelical church, on the surface. But there are sub-cultural distinctives that are worth noting and noticing.

Pastor Wilson Wang planted Renew Church in Fullerton, California, with a vision "to make followers of Jesus through missional communities that display the gospel through words, life together and sacrificial love." With the support of Ambassador Church as its mother church (or sending church), Renew Church has become more diverse since its inception, with about 35% to 40% non-Asians in weekly attendance. At an Exponential church planting conference workshop, Pastor Wilson described how the group-orientation from his Chinese-American upbringing has contributed most significantly to the community life of Renew Church:

> The underlying trait that is inherent for many Asian Americans brings together valuable cultural elements from both East and West, that is, the group-oriented collective mentality and being concerned for the whole group without having to explicitly say it out loud. This bonds the next generation Asian Americans with non-Asian millennials.

This is seen in how Renew Church does its outreach which is essential to the survival of a church plant. They found that when their small groups outreach as a team, as a missional community, it was more inviting and effective. A typical American church would exhort its members to be evangelistic by being a missionary to invite friends, neighbors, and co-workers to church events, which is a more individualistic mindset. Instead, outreach was baked into how small groups are done at Renew Church, and small groups meet and reach out right where they lived, in apartment complexes and neighborhoods. For someone without any church background, going to a smaller gathering with a neighbor would be less threatening than a big event.

Doing life together is another aspect of how this group-orientation helps build relationships. For a typical majority-culture church goer, worship service tends to be an event on the calendar, where you go to church for 90 minutes and everyone scatters on their own way for the rest of the day.

For Asian Americans who have attended ethnic Asian churches in the past, being a part of church was an all-day affair because church served as a community center for first generation Asians to connect through their native language and culture. That's partly why lunch programs are commonly found in ethnic Asian churches. In a church like Renew, this value for community and relationship beyond the worship service resides deeply in its culture. People worship together and stay afterwards for another hour or two to fellowship, then head out to eat together. In similar fashion, during the course of the week, they do life together by going to the movies and cafes, visiting each other's homes, and meeting as small groups. This kind of group cohesion is a part of everyday relationships rather than a church-mandated program.

A third way that this group-orientation comes into play is the instinct for inclusion. Asian Americans have an awareness for people who are left out. Whether it's during worship service or during a fellowship time, Pastor Wilson values a culture where every person in the room is engaged in a conversation. If one person is standing alone, someone will come along, start a conversation, and extend an invitation for community. For example: "Hey, why don't you come to lunch with us." Or, "If you're not doing anything this afternoon, come and join us for basketball."

These values of community in living missionally and doing life together come out of Pastor Wilson's ethnic Chinese church experience and community-oriented Asian culture. He has found that it's resonated with millennials longing for church to be more than a Sunday service; but rather, an honest and interconnected community.

CAVEAT

The characteristics listed above of next generation multi-Asian churches are descriptive and not prescriptive. They were not systematically identified through data analysis from a survey or interviews. They are merely a broad paintbrush stroke of things I've noticed through my networking. As an Asian American of Chinese descent myself, I may not be aware of additional characteristics that someone who is non-Asian would more easily notice. That's one of the things about a cultural context that makes it hard to describe by someone who is immersed in it—it's like a fish being asked to describe the water it's swimming in.

While the examples are mostly Asian Americans from East Asian descent (Korean, Chinese, Japanese), next generation Asian American churches, pastors, and ministry leaders are rising up from Southeast Asian and South Asian backgrounds too. The Southeast Asian Catalyst has hosted national leadership conferences every other year since 2006 for next generation Southeast Asian Christian ministry leaders from ethnic backgrounds like Hmong, Mien, Lao, Vietnamese, Thai, Cambodian, and others. The Advance Initiative was launched in 2015 to equip next generation Asian Indian American church planters to launch healthy multiethnic churches.

These next generation multi-Asian churches are showing us creative ways to reach more people in the younger generations, both Asian and non-Asian. Because these churches are agile and adaptable, they're doing ministry in different ways than the traditional ethnic Asian churches. I think they give us a picture of what future Asian American churches would look like, as many indicators show that existing ethnic Asian church models are not effective in reaching the fast-growing Asian American population that's on the brink of doubling in our lifetime.

·

CHAPTER 7
WHY WE NEED THESE NEW CHURCHES

Church planting may be particularly challenging in an Asian American church context for a couple of reasons. Many of us who have been a Christian for a long time have experienced a church split, where a new church is formed as a result of unresolved conflict. Whether the conflict was justified or not, it obviously was not resolved. The prominence of shame in Asian cultures can make reconciliation particularly difficult, even when the Bible clearly teaches how the heart of the Gospel is about the ministry of reconciliation (2 Corinthians 5:18), both with God and with one another.

In addition to contextual challenges, church planting in general is difficult for anyone in any context. It's not for the faint of heart. Yet, we must take on these challenges if we're going to be faithful to the mission of God for our generation and the next generation, because there's a lot at stake.

When I was part of a church planting team back in 1997, there were very few resources to help navigate the many challenges and the hard work of planting a church. We faced more risk and uncertainty for what we were doing, so we had to learn by trial and error, and metaphorically speaking, building the plane as we begin to fly.

Today, there are all kinds of resources: a variety of books published on the subject, websites with free resources and online training, conferences (such as Exponential), and plenty more of church planting networks too. There is a short list of these resources available for you at multiasian.church/planting.

There are many reasons for planting new churches, too many to name. I will provide an overview of these reasons in three categories using Pastor Ray Chang's presentation:[50]

BIBLICAL

First and foremost, all that we do as a church and followers of Christ must be based on the teachings found in the Bible. Here are some of the classic Bible passages about the importance of the church—as is, without commentary:

Matthew 16:18-19
And I tell you, you are Peter, and on this rock I will build my church, and the gates of hell shall not prevail against it. I will give you the keys of the kingdom of heaven, and whatever you bind on earth shall be bound in heaven, and whatever you loose on earth shall be loosed in heaven.

Matthew 28:18-20
And Jesus came and said to them, "All authority in heaven and on earth has been given to me. Go therefore and make disciples of all nations, baptizing them in the name of the Father and of the Son and of the Holy Spirit, teaching them to observe all that I have commanded you. And behold, I am with you always, to the end of the age."

Acts 1:8
But you will receive power when the Holy Spirit has come upon you, and you will be my witnesses in Jerusalem and in all Judea and Samaria, and to the end of the earth.

Acts 2:42-47
And they devoted themselves to the apostles' teaching and the

fellowship, to the breaking of bread and the prayers. And awe came upon every soul, and many wonders and signs were being done through the apostles. And all who believed were together and had all things in common. And they were selling their possessions and belongings and distributing the proceeds to all, as any had need. And day by day, attending the temple together and breaking bread in their homes, they received their food with glad and generous hearts, praising God and having favor with all the people. And the Lord added to their number day by day those who were being saved.

Ephesians 4:11-16
And he gave the apostles, the prophets, the evangelists, the shepherds and teachers, to equip the saints for the work of ministry, for building up the body of Christ, until we all attain to the unity of the faith and of the knowledge of the Son of God, to mature manhood, to the measure of the stature of the fullness of Christ, so that we may no longer be children, tossed to and fro by the waves and carried about by every wind of doctrine, by human cunning, by craftiness in deceitful schemes. Rather, speaking the truth in love, we are to grow up in every way into him who is the head, into Christ, from whom the whole body, joined and held together by every joint with which it is equipped, when each part is working properly, makes the body grow so that it builds itself up in love.

After reading these passages, you may be wondering if you missed something because you didn't see the words: "Go ye therefore and plant new churches." And you are correct, those exact words are not written in the Bible black and white.

However, when these Bible passages are read and synthesized together with other teachings in the New Testament about the church, they bring out one important principle: a healthy community needs to have a healthy structure. For example, it's very helpful to tie a tomato plant to a wooden stake so it can stand tall; or, the bones of my skeleton provides the structure to hold together my whole body. Where it was wise, helpful, and strategic, churches have changed their structures in order to facilitate health and growth. Over the course of church history, the local church has taken on many different organizational structures, theological frameworks, and governance models. In other words, different structures are needed at different times in different places for different peoples. We have a responsibility to create an environment where disciples from different backgrounds can grow into Christ-like maturity.

PERSONAL

To plant a new church is not merely a human endeavor. It is a spiritual battle, and it must be grounded in a solid foundation of faith, self-awareness, discernment, and wisdom. It is hard work, very hard work. Some liken it to running a startup business; yet church is more than a business. It has a spiritual aspect, a burden, that businesses don't carry. It faces real world challenges plus an additional spiritual dimension on top of that.

I'd like to address the church planter for this section. A church planter must have a God-given conviction to clearly answer this question which is frequently asked: why do *you* want to plant a *new church* in *this community* at *this time*? There are lots of external reasons why church planting is needed. But the church planter has to look within and get to the heart of the matter. You'd want to be honest with yourself in checking your motives.

Notice the underlined four parts of this question: why you and not someone else? Why a church plant rather than another ministry within an existing church? Why this city or neighborhood or people group instead of another? Why now and not later? A church planter needs to be crystal clear on this "why" question before he can effectively recruit leaders, workers, prayer supporters, and potential donors.

For a church planter to answer, "God told me so," it can come across evasive, or seen as a naive leap of faith without much discernment. Proverbs 15:22 says, "Without counsel plans fail, but with many advisers they succeed." Planting a church without thinking through it thoroughly is unwise. Consequences may include disillusionment of other lives, and even the church planter's own life and marriage. It's not good stewardship and bordering irresponsibility.

Who can you be honest with about why you want to get into church planting? Who do you let into your life, to speak to you honestly and lovingly about your strengths and weaknesses? It's a good spiritual exercise to open yourself up to God and a couple of trusted friends, and go before God in prayer and echo the words in Psalm 139:23-24 says, "Search me, O God, and know my heart! Try me and know my thoughts! And see if there be any grievous way in me, and lead me in the way everlasting!"

Additionally, ask yourself, what is motivating you? There is a vast possibility of motives and motivations: compassion for the lost, desire to preach, desire to expand God's kingdom, wanting to prove something, needing for more churches, no other opportunities for an existing church position, burden to reach specific people, can't get along with other Christians, wanting to do your own thing, personal theological agenda, etc., etc., etc.

It is better and wiser to approach church planting with a sense of calling from God and a clear conscience before God and others. Be sure to include your spouse in this exploration and decision, because church planting isn't just a day job, it will significantly impact your marriage and your family.

For those considering getting involved in planting churches, here are some simple steps to follow before you begin: research and learn from the resources, networks, and training that are readily available to you. Choose one to work with that fits with your sending church's philosophy of ministry. Then prayerfully identify a chosen few from your own congregation who have a heart for church planting. Connect them to the resources that will help with the rest of the journey.

PRACTICAL

Lastly, there are practical reasons that church planting is valuable for expanding the Kingdom of God and helping more people find their way back to God:

1. Better evangelism – statistics show that the most effective evangelistic method is planting new churches. Pastor Ralph Moore has been a part of planting 30 churches that have reproduced more than 2,200 churches worldwide. He has noted, "New churches provide superior results. Some denominations have found as much as 80% of their conversion growth comes from new churches."

2. Population growth – the numbers clearly show that church growth has been unable to keep up with population growth. Researcher David Olson noted in his book, The American Church in Crisis, that while the population of the United States grew by 52 million from 1990-2006, the total worship attendance in American churches remain unchanged.

3. Ministry opportunity with immigrants – Asian Americans now have the highest immigration rate out of all racial ethnic groups. As mentioned in Chapter 3, when people move to a new location or a new country, they're more receptive to the Gospel and it's one of the best opportunities for churches to serve these immigrants practically.

These are all compelling reasons for planting new churches. However, it doesn't mean that your church should jump into it right away. Similarly, not everyone can be a church planter, as much as one believes in the importance of it. Based on the entrepreneurial skills required in church planting, only about 10-15% of pastors have the natural abilities common to most successful church planters. Undoubtedly God can do much more than our human limitations; but most of the time, we can fulfill His plan in our lives more completely by using the gifts, abilities, and desires that He has given precisely in each of us, faithfully.

For a more thorough discussion and understanding on why we need new churches, and how to actually plant a church practically, please visit the resources listed at multiasian.church/planting. I also recommend the resources of two networks: Ambassador Network and ReGenerant Network. I am a team member of both of these networks, dedicated to resourcing churches to be multiplying, multi-ethnic, and missional. Ambassador Network provides coaching, consulting, and training to existing churches and new churches, while ReGenerant Network has a tighter focus on planting Asian American churches, a simpler term for what I've described as next generation multi-Asian churches.

There's yet another challenge that makes church planting difficult, because the idea for church planting is unknown and uncommon. When something is unknown, it can result in suspicion and rejection.

Pastor David Hsu is the senior pastor of West Houston Chinese Church. Pastor David is particularly gifted to lead this bi-lingual Chinese church because of his fluency in both English and Mandarin Chinese. Pastor Ted Law served alongside Pastor David in the English ministry faithfully and effectively for eight years until he began to sense a vision from God to plant a new church to reach a diverse multiethnic community in urban Houston.

Pastor David and the church leadership prayed together to confirm Pastor Ted's new calling and planned a healthy transition over the span of a year. With the help of denomination support, the church prepared to send out Pastor Ted to plant with full blessings, financial support, and a core group of 40 people.

Even when the relationships between West Houston's pastors and church leadership were healthy, there were still a few members who did not understand the reasons for this church plant. They could only view it as a "church split." They were suspicious in part due to painful church experiences in the past, and understandably so.

With good teaching and time for healing, the overall process was overwhelmingly positive for the church as a whole. This is a good example of an ethnic Asian church that is striving to be faithful in furthering God's Kingdom, demonstrating healthy partnership and reproduction.

IT'S HEALTHY TO REPRODUCE

Many churches start by reaching one demographic, one generation, one particular ethnicity. But it's not healthy to stay there, i.e., becoming sterile and stagnant. Healthy things grow and reproduce. Every church is given the mission to bear witness to the Gospel of Jesus Christ, and the Great

Commission is to make disciples of all nationalities. Let's determine the next steps we need to take in God's plan during our time and our generation.

This overview on the importance of church planting sets the table for a follow-up question: Why do we need next generation multi-Asian churches, in particular? Why can't churches just be Gospel-centered and preach the Bible, leaving the results up to God? This will be my topic for the next chapter.

CHAPTER 8
WHY MULTI-ASIAN CHURCHES

The typical Asian American church will bring together people from two ends of the cultural spectrum, from the East and the West. When an Asian American church starts by reaching first generation immigrants from Asia, naturally over the course of time, immigrant parents would have children who are raised in America.

WHEN EAST MEETS WEST

For people acculturated with an Eastern perspective, first generation Asians are accustomed to a high-context with values in traditions, family, filial piety, respect for authority, harmony, honor, protocol, social status, loyalty, and being group-oriented. For people acculturated in a Western society, next generation Asian Americans are socialized in a low-context culture with values in individualism, directness, assertiveness, casual informality, egalitarian, mobility, and results-oriented. (This broad overview is only intended to contrast some of the cultural differences and not to be used as a guide for cultural competency.)

Bringing people together with these widely divergent cultural differences can be particularly challenging; misunderstandings and conflicts can easily arise. Additionally, these conflicts can disrupt the social order of generational and familial relationships, which become intensely painful and shameful. For example, what a next generation Asian American intends as an honest inquiry or question for clarification may be perceived by a first generation Asian American as disrespect for questioning authority.

Allow me to share a personal experience: when I graduated from Dallas Theological Seminary and went into full-time pastoral ministry at a traditional Chinese church, I thought my seminary training could be applied right away. I was thoroughly mistaken. I was completely clueless to the cultural context of the traditional ethnic Chinese church, even though I had grown up in a Chinese family with traditional parents and brothers. I looked Asian on the outside, but much of my thinking was very Americanized.

In my desperation, I wasn't able to find a book that I could get answers on Chinese culture, like I could with many other subjects I studied in seminary. In my attempt to be teachable, I asked people to explain how things were done or why things were the way they were. But those I approached were unable to use words to explain Chinese culture to me.

I remembered my interactions with an older Chinese man who had shown me kindness by taking time to listen to my struggling to understand Chinese culture. He didn't respond with a lot of explanation, because that's a rather direct form of communication. Instead, he encouraged me to read a book titled *Animal Farm* by George Orwell. When we discussed the book after I read it, he implied how the allegorical stories in the book has similarities to some of the people dynamics I was experiencing. I had learned from a master at indirect communication.

Through that interaction and many others since then, I've come to realize that culture is not something to be explained; culture is something that has to be experienced. Culture is more than language, behaviors, beliefs, and values. This helpful diagram, known as the "cultural iceberg," illustrates a smaller number of cultural elements above the water and a larger number of cultural elements under the water:[51]

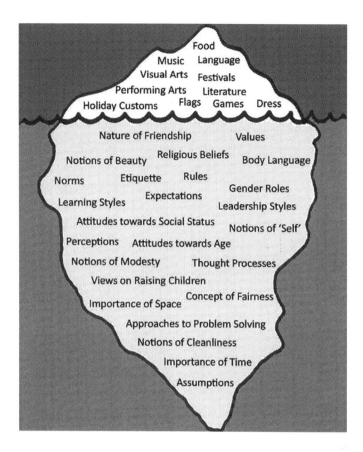

Above the water are "surface culture" elements, like food, music, language, and literature; these are easier to understand because they're seen and heard. Below the water are "deep culture" elements like communication styles, body language, and etiquette, which in Asian cultures are particularly nuanced and harder to grasp without being experienced.

BICULTURAL BENEFITS

During their formative teenage years, Asian Americans often wrestle with their sense of identity, struggling to belong with their Asian community or being fully accepted as an all-American person. It's fairly common for next generation Asian Americans to experience feelings of being "second class" or "not fitting in." On the one hand, shamed for not speaking the Asian language well. On the other hand, Asian Americans are stereotyped by racial insensitivities or mistaken for a different Asian ethnicity, being ignorantly asked the subsequent question, "Where are you really from?" I've been there myself, so I can sincerely say that I've felt that pain.

However, rather than being limited by these challenges and struggles, I believe that being Asian American is "more than," not "less than."[52] While some Asian Americans may not fully identify with Asians or Americans, we can draw from our bi-cultural backgrounds to bring out the best from both cultures and to better navigate in a multicultural world to make our unique contribution. This is not an easy thing to achieve, as it has taken me years to come to this realization myself. Instead of fighting the cultures as if they were constraining, embrace the opportunity to develop cross-cultural competencies.

Because culture is more caught than taught, we who have the lived experiences of being immersed in two very different cultures—Asian and American—are a huge asset in a multiethnic and multicultural context of America, and the global village of the world as well. We were born into an immigrant Asian family context which instills Asian cultural values, at the same time conversant in American values through school, work, and relationships with peers.

And that's what is uniquely special about multi-Asian churches. They are a particular kind of multi-ethnic churches that have the valuable contribution of Asian Americans. First, let's go back to the Bible to discover God's heart for what He wants in His church.

BIBLICAL MANDATE FOR MULTIETHNIC CHURCHES

Why do we need multiethnic churches when diversity is so hard to achieve? The reason is not to be more politically correct, or to address our society's need for racial reconciliation. The reasons for multiethnic churches are clearly biblical, theological, and practical. Everything we do as Christ-followers and churches must be grounded in what the Bible teaches.

Pastor Mark DeYmaz, who pastors Mosaic Church of Central Arkansas,[53] has authored two books on this subject, *Building a Healthy Multi-ethnic*

Church: Mandate, Commitments and Practices of a Diverse Congregation
and *Leading a Healthy Multi-Ethnic Church: Seven Common Challenges
and How to Overcome Them.* The second book is co-authored with Harry
Li, an Asian American pastor who ministers together with Pastor DeYmaz.
In a Leadership Journal interview, Pastor DeYmaz summarized the biblical
mandate for a multiethnic church:[54]

> Christ envisions the multi-ethnic church on the night before
> he dies (John 17:20-23), so that the world will know God's love
> and believe.
>
> Luke describes the model at Antioch (Acts 11:19-26; 13:1ff.), the first
> mega, missional, and multi-ethnic community of faith and the most
> influential church in the New Testament.
>
> Paul prescribes unity and diversity for the local church in his letter
> to the Ephesians, where his theme is "the unity of the church for
> the sake of the Gospel."

The Bible can speak for itself. Here's three of the key passages:

John 17:20-23
"I do not ask for these only, but also for those who will believe in
me through their word, that they may all be one, just as you, Father,
are in me, and I in you, that they also may be in us, so that the
world may believe that you have sent me. The glory that you have
given me I have given to them, that they may be one even as we are
one, I in them and you in me, that they may become perfectly one,
so that the world may know that you sent me and loved them even
as you loved me."

Ephesians 3:1-10
For this reason I, Paul, a prisoner for Christ Jesus on behalf of you
Gentiles—assuming that you have heard of the stewardship of God's
grace that was given to me for you, how the mystery was made
known to me by revelation, as I have written briefly. When you read
this, you can perceive my insight into the mystery of Christ, which
was not made known to the sons of men in other generations as

it has now been revealed to his holy apostles and prophets by the Spirit. This mystery is that the Gentiles are fellow heirs, members of the same body, and partakers of the promise in Christ Jesus through the gospel. Of this gospel I was made a minister according to the gift of God's grace, which was given me by the working of his power. To me, though I am the very least of all the saints, this grace was given, to preach to the Gentiles the unsearchable riches of Christ, and to bring to light for everyone what is the plan of the mystery hidden for ages in God who created all things, so that through the church the manifold wisdom of God might now be made known to the rulers and authorities in the heavenly places.

Revelation 7:9-10
After this I looked, and behold, a great multitude that no one could number, from every nation, from all tribes and peoples and languages, standing before the throne and before the Lamb, clothed in white robes, with palm branches in their hands, and crying out with a loud voice, "Salvation belongs to our God who sits on the throne, and to the Lamb!"

The Ephesians 3 passage clearly explains that the mystery of the Gospel is revealed to us, that the Gospel is for everyone, both Jews and Gentiles, both Asian and Americans. In fact, for every nation, every tribe, every people group, and every language. The Good News brings everyone riches, promises, hope, and peace.

This is the power of the Gospel on full display for the world to see. The multiethnic church is the best showcase of people coming together across racial, ethnic, class, socio-economic, and generational differences. And when people worship together because they've been reconciled to God and to one another, the world will know God's love and believe in Him; this is what Jesus prayed for in John 17. The best showcase of human diversity is not the Olympics or the United Nations. The best showcase of human diversity unified as one is the local church, where people are worshipping together and living peacefully with one another, for now and forever.

If the multiethnic church is the biblical mandate, then why are there so many Bible-teaching churches not multiethnic and racially diverse? According to this quote attributed to Martin Luther King, Jr., "Eleven o'clock on Sunday morning is the most segregated hour of America."

Indeed, years after the Civil Rights movement of the 1960s, the American church is still largely segregated. Sociologists define a church as being multiethnic when the congregation has at least 20% diversity. The 2012 National Congregations Study results show that 20% attend churches where no single racial or ethnic group makes up at least 80% of the congregation.[55]

To be fair, legitimately, a local church could be mono-cultural because the demographics of its locality is not diverse, or due to language limitations of an ethnic church for immigrants. But in an increasingly diversified America, that is a shrinking reality in almost every state in the United States.

Dozens of books and research have been published about multiethnic churches, explaining the many complicated reasons why there are so few of them. These reasons include the systemic racial problems, social injustices, homogeneous church growth pragmatics, and cultural blind spots.

There are also simple reasons why there's only a few true diverse multiethnic churches: It's natural for people to only want to be around people like themselves. And it's normal for people to stay away from anything uncomfortable; I know I like wearing t-shirts that are only 100% cotton.

As I'm writing this chapter, I just finished a phone conversation with a Caucasian pastor in the Dallas Fort Worth area, describing his experience with leading his church to diversify. The church went from primarily being Caucasian to having 30% minority during the past couple of years. It was not an easy process; it was met with resistance. Even though the church is very active in cross-cultural missions overseas, church members said they were uncomfortable with the increasing diversity in their church. Their resistance was not due to the variety of races, but because of different cultures. What's disruptive is not that people looked different from one another; but rather, it's how people talked, ate, behaved, and worshipped differently.

The Gospel—the heart of God, calls every church to be a supernatural witness for all peoples, not limiting itself to one locality or one language. Every church is to be a supernatural work of God, which starts in one place and progressively takes steps toward fulfilling the God-given mission to spread the Gospel to the ends of the earth.

Within the limited scope of this book, I will address two topics related to how the local church can be fulfilling the Gospel mandate more completely: contextualization and multi-Asian churches.

IMPORTANCE OF CONTEXTUALIZATION

Have you noticed that the Bible has not just one, but four Gospels about Jesus Christ? Why wasn't one Gospel enough for everyone? Matthew was written for the Jews. Mark was written for the Romans. Luke wrote to the Greeks, and John was writing with the Gentiles in mind. In a similar fashion, different expressions of local churches are strategic for reaching different demographics.

Because the Bible has four Gospels of Jesus Christ, we get four different perspectives of the same true story which make the story richer and more meaningful. No one would say that we need only one of the Gospels. We need the entire Bible: the Old Testament and the New Testament, because they are both valuable to our entire life. As it is written in 2 Timothy 3:16-17, "All Scripture is breathed out by God and profitable for teaching, for reproof, for correction, and for training in righteousness, that the man of God may be complete, equipped for every good work."

Pastor Tim Keller eloquently explained the importance of contextualization in his book, *Preaching: Communicating Faith in an Age of Skepticism,*

> "The moment you open your mouth, many things—your cadence, accent, vocabulary, illustrations and ways of reasoning, and the way you express emotions—make you culturally more accessible to some people and force others to stretch and work harder to understand or even pay attention to you. No one can present a culture-free formulation of biblical truth."[56]

Pastor Tim Keller has also become an active Twitter user in recent years.[57] This is a short curated list of tweets that further expounds his view on the necessity of contextualization:

> Everyone contextualizes – but few think much about how they are doing it.
> https://twitter.com/timkellernyc/status/697895952590491648

> When you open your mouth and speak in English you are making the gospel hearable to some and not others. That's contextualization.
> https://twitter.com/timkellernyc/status/698505638540922880

> Contextualization is giving people the answers the gospel gives to the questions they have.
> https://twitter.com/timkellernyc/status/680010233201180672

> Sound contextualization shows people how the plotlines of the stories of their lives can only find a happy ending in Christ.
> https://twitter.com/timkellernyc/status/599605297834020864

> "One of the biggest barriers to effective contextualization is the invisibility of our own cultural assumptions."
> @timkellernyc #CenterChurch
> https://twitter.com/M_Breezy215/status/358802937948020736

> "We adapt and contextualize in order to speak the truth in love, to both care and to confront." @timkellernyc #preaching
> https://twitter.com/dalehuntington/status/628946705551994884

> "To reach people we must appreciate and adapt to their culture, but we must also challenge and confront it" @timkellernyc #Contextualization
> https://twitter.com/MichelGaleano/status/708326915233288193

For a more thorough treatment of contextualization, I highly recommend Tim Keller's book, *Center Church: Doing Balanced, Gospel-Centered Ministry in Your City*, in which he devotes four chapters to contextualization. Chapter 10 on Active Contextualization is available as a free PDF download at timothykeller.com/books/center-church.

So it is in this multicultural diverse world in which the church must contextualize its Gospel expression as a community of faith. Furthermore, to be faithful in a multicultural society, we must become more aware of our own cultural lenses and biases in order to know how we influence and impact others, both those who are similar and those who are not.

How can you and your church better contextualize for the world today? In one sense, you and your church already contextualizes based on your life experience and culture. That's where we all start.

Yet, the Gospel calls all of us to participate in the work of God "to the ends of the earth." In multicultural America, that is easy for us to do because people from all around the world are coming here. Asian Americans already know that innately because the immigration story is right here in our immediate family history. Current events have also raised our awareness of immigration from many other nationalities and racial ethnic groups. To reach people from around the world in many American cities and suburbs, we simply need to go across the street or to the neighborhood across town.

This is why you and I must do the work of contextualization, so that we can grow our capacity to share the Gospel beyond our own cultural comfort zone. And to do that, there's no easy way, no recipe, or online course; it is plain hard work to learn something totally different.

Here are a few tips on learning contextualization: Have the attitude of a student and a learner. Get a guide or translator when going to a new people group nearby or across town. If you don't have one, befriend someone over meals. Sharing a meal together had so much more meaning during Old Testament times. It is an integral part of crossing cultures. With a sincere and respectful curiosity, ask good questions and be a great listener. People of all cultures have a born instinct to sense your sincerity. At the top of this chapter, I mentioned how culture is something you have to experience. As your friendship grows, you'll earn to trust, take more risks, and make mistakes as you learn how to communicate better cross-culturally.

Contextualization is not just the message of the Gospel and the words we use to communicate. Contextualization also affects our theology and our ecclesiology. Recent scholarship is surfacing the subject of global theology. It is beginning to reveal how much our theology and ecclesiology have been solely shaped by European cultures and Western civilization. Some of this may be attributed to the sovereignty of God and how the Gospel has spread during the past twenty centuries. But as the center of Christianity is shifting to the South and the East, we are beginning to discover new perspectives from South American, African, and Asian Christian leaders.

This is where I believe the multiethnic churches have the potential to more fully express the Gospel in a multicultural way. The multi-ethnic church can be the best context for people to grow together in a community of trusted relationships in order to caringly challenge cultural blind spots and experientially learn one another's cultures. Discussions of faith and race can often feel rather awkward and uncomfortable, because most of us don't have practice in navigating multiple cultures or respectful conversations cross-culturally. Multiethnic church can be the answer—a safe place to appreciate the differences and work out the contextualizing of the Gospel for their community while participating in the mission of God for the world.

WHY MULTI-ASIAN CHURCHES

American history has been racialized through its government policies which supported slavery, discrimination, prejudice, and other injustices. Even in the history of American churches, there was the formation of denominations along racial lines. For example, the Baptists split into two denominations in 1845 over slavery. The north became the American Baptists; the south became the Southern Baptists. Over time, the Southern Baptist Convention has become and remains the largest Protestant denomination in America today. Yet, it wasn't until 1995 that Southern Baptist officials formally renounced the church's support of slavery and segregation. Thus, in this American context, a majority portion of the development of multiethnic churches has involved the racial reconciliation between white and black, Caucasians and African Americans. We've made some progress, but we still have a long way to go.

With this new phenomena I call multi-Asian churches, I believe this gives the American church another way to bring hope and healing to many. Multi-Asian churches are a different kind of multiethnic church. It is led by a next generation Asian American pastor. The bi-cultural experience of an Asian American can be leveraged as a head start for acquiring new skills in crossing cultures and for facilitating cross-cultural dialogue.

Perhaps due to the fact that Asian Americans have a different narrative in our part of the American history, we have something different to contribute. We don't have a long history of racial tension such as the one between white and black that's lasted generations and resurfaced in recent violence in cities like Ferguson, Baltimore, and Dallas, with no end in sight.

These racial tension and systemic inequalities between black and white could have resulted in everything being stuck. Maybe we can try a different approach to do an end run around the stalemate and possibly discover a new way forward. Asian Americans have the experience of mediating reconciliation indirectly and relationally by coming alongside of contentious parties. This is a contrast to having everyone directly air their grievances out loud and then asking for forgiveness. It's parallel to the difference between acupuncture and invasive surgery.

Having a mediator to facilitate reconciliation in broken relationships is common practice in the biblical cultures of the Old and New Testaments as well. So in the context of racial tension in American history, then, perhaps a table that's hosted by an Asian American could facilitate healthier progress in ways we've yet to experience.

Multi-Asian churches are also best contextualized to reach next generation Asian Americans. Some next generation Asian Americans have a difficult time feeling at home in an ethnic Asian church or the mainstream American church; both of those tend to be too homogeneous. A multi-Asian church can be a more inviting place for next generation Asian Americans and non-Asians alike, because its ethos of bi-cultural elasticity can accommodate more diversity. When I've experienced a healthy multi-Asian church, I describe it as entering a church community not having to explain myself so much, because I'm with people who have shared experience and empathy for my bi-cultural background.

Let me share an example of a multi-Asian church that's developed a multi-ethnic church family. In 2012, Pastor Drew Hyun gathered weekly with a group of people, eating, praying, and dreaming about starting a family of churches in New York City. Hope Church NYC launched first in Astoria. And now, 4 years later, Hope Church NYC has a family of churches in five diverse neighborhoods across New York city: Roosevelt Island, Midtown Manhattan, Long Island, Bayside in Queens, and Brooklyn. Each of these churches are called Hope Church and share the same vision and core values to lead people into a transforming relationship with Jesus and a community of faith. Yet each church is autonomous and independently-governed so they're fully empowered to lead and serve their own communities as they discern best. In a place like New York City, planting neighborhood churches right where people live allows the transforming power of community to continually seep into their lives every day rather than once a week on Sundays. Pastor Drew Hyun (a next generation Korean American) has intentionally directed the Hope Church family to empower minorities in planting diverse churches. The pastors of the other Hope Churches include a New York native second generation Puerto Rican, a Korean-American, an Indian-American, an African-American, and two Caucasians.

In May of 2016, Pastor Drew was part of launching an urban church planting network called the New City Network that hosted its first conference, the New City Gathering. This gathering consisted of 170 diverse church planters and practitioners from around the country. Amongst other topics, the heart for launching diverse church communities was emphasized and discussed at length.

ALL KINDS OF CHURCHES FOR ALL PEOPLES

"It takes all kinds of churches to reach all kinds of people," said Pastor Rick Warren. In this cultural climate of America that's becoming more and more antagonistic to Christianity, I'm not inclined to waste my resources on discernment ministries and their watchdog blogs, or developing the best arguments for the right theology, methodology and model of ministry. I would encourage church leaders to be thoroughly convinced from the Scriptures on how to do ministry and how to organize their Biblical understanding into a coherent theology. Churches need to have firm convictions but we don't need to be wasting time being contentious with one another. Let me address a couple of common issues that surfaced in my conversations with pastors and church leaders.

Some pastors say, "We just need churches that preach the Gospel and leave the results up to God." Yes, absolutely, we need Gospel-preaching churches. And, we need to realize that everything speaks: what and how we preach, the communication style and language used, how we choose and sing the worship songs, the way we relate, the decor of the worship center, and so much more. There's a lot going on in a church than merely its statement of beliefs or doctrines. Some church leaders like to quote, "The message never changes, but methods can change." My encouragement here is to be thoughtful and strategic on how your church does its ministry in order to evaluate your ministry effectiveness. And when something is not effective, be willing to make changes. We want churches that are both faithful **and** fruitful.

What about ethnic Asian churches? Yes, there's an obvious need for the ethnic Asian church to reach and minister to first generation immigrants from Asia in the language that they can understand. There's also the call for all churches to participate in God's work to reach all peoples. If not for the missionaries sent to cross the seas to share the Gospel in Asia, there wouldn't be Asian Christians. There are still unengaged unreached people groups around the world with no Bible, no churches, and no Christians, and ethnic Asian churches can make a unique contribution in sharing the Gospel there.

Many pastors in ethnic Asian churches face the challenges of ministering to the next generation English-speaking Asian Americans. The question I hear most often is: "How do we keep our children in church?" It's natural to want their children to keep the faith by belonging to the same church that would have a familiar family-oriented Asian culture. And "[God] is able to do immeasurably more than all we ask or imagine, according to his power that is at work within us" (Ephesians 3:20, NIV).

May I suggest a different perspective that would be more helpful. Consider these more Gospel-oriented questions to look beyond the challenges and see the opportunities: how can our church be a place where our children can bring their friends? What does God want us to do in our city? Or who does God want us to reach beyond our own ethnicity? I think if churches become the answers to these kinds of questions, they will get to keep their children and receive so much more. When we join in God's adventure of living by faith, churches will not be irrelevant or boring (cf. John 10:10).

In the next chapter, I will introduce stories of multi-generational churches and how they're reaching next generation Asian Americans and beyond.

CHAPTER 9

CHURCHES THAT LAST FOR GENERATIONS

Churches have existed for many generations, beginning with Jesus Christ, who said "I will build my church," through the apostles and disciples back in the first century. These early churches were planted in Ephesus, Thessalonica, Galatia, Philippi, Corinth, and other cities. We have books in the New Testament written to those churches called the epistles. It would be similar to how we communicate with email newsletters and blog posts today, but much easier I might add, as a link on social media or clicking forward in your email inbox.

But where are those churches now? They no longer exist. This is not to say that it's impossible for a church to last a hundred generations, but it definitely takes significant effort to have a church last more than one generation. It is not going to happen accidentally or incidentally.

On Pinterest, I've curated a photo collection of ex-church buildings. Particularly in many parts of Europe and some places in the United States, there are now growing numbers of buildings which used to be churches and have since been renovated for other usage. They have been converted into lofts, apartments, exquisite homes, libraries, restaurants, banks, community centers, or real estate developments. No longer are they houses of worship and prayer to the living God.

In Southeast Washington DC, there's a building that served as home to Central Baptist Church from 1997 to 2005. Today, it is Muhammad Mosque No. 4, the Mid-Atlantic Regional Headquarters of the Nation of Islam. While it is true that "church" is the people and not the building, the building is still a testimony and a visible witness to where people gathered to worship the living God. Massive cathedrals were built in past generations with a purpose to help illiterate people to experience and understand the grandeur of God.

An ex-church building is a sobering picture of what could be the future of any church, if the church leadership does not take strategic steps to prepare for its future by reaching the next generation. In other words, such church can be just one generation from extinction. Let's pause for a moment and let that sink in.

> **Judges 2:7**
> And the people served the Lord all the days of Joshua, and all the days of the elders who outlived Joshua, who had seen all the great work that the Lord had done for Israel.

> **Judges 2:10**
> And all that generation also were gathered to their fathers. And there arose another generation after them who did not know the Lord or the work that he had done for Israel.

Churches have a natural life span; most churches are planted to reach young adults and young families. Those young families have children who grow up and eventually leave home for college. And as their founding members begin to pass on one by one, the church's vitality naturally declines. One church expert has noted that the average lifespan of a church is about the same as that of the average human being: 70 years.[58]

For a more thorough explanation about a natural life cycle that all churches go through, take a look at this free eBook by Geoff Surratt titled, "Measuring the Orchard: Changing the Scorecard on Church Growth."

Some churches are able to continue on beyond one generation because its church leaders held on to "the faith that was once for all delivered to the saints" (Jude 1:3) rather than hanging on to traditions per se. As mentioned in previous chapter, instead of asking the question, "How do we keep our children in church?" I think a better question would be: how do we reach our children's friends? Or how do we reach the next generation? Churches that recognize the responsibility to reach the next generation are the ones also willing to recognize when to make necessary adjustments in order to stay current with the next generation.

In the remainder of this chapter, I will describe three accounts of churches who took big steps of faith in making adjustments so that the future generation can experience a vibrant faith practical and relevant for them; hence, the church able to continue its mission. A word of thanks to all three churches for granting permission for their history to be published; their histories are presented in their own words, in honor of their legacy.

The first church history is from Evergreen Baptist Church of Los Angeles, now 91 years old. Evergreen has served multiple generations over the years: Starting with first-generation Japanese immigrants, onto English-speaking Japanese-Americans, multiple Asian American ethnicities, and now a multi-ethnic and multi-racial congregation.

> In 1925, nearsighted young Japanese Pastor Haruye Shibata boldly accepted the challenge from the Los Angeles Baptist City Mission Society and steamed slowly across the Pacific to a hostile denizen known as Boyle Heights (East LA). His first converts were the Issei (first-generation Japanese-American) pioneers. None of them were wealthy, but they soon learned the joy of sacrificial giving. Boyle Heights Baptist Church eventually became a special gathering place for them and their families.

> By 1938 there was a fast-growing population of English-speaking congregants, and Rev. Jitsuo Morikawa, a young Japanese-Canadian pastor, accepted the call to be their pastor, while also serving a Japanese-American congregations in Terminal Island in the South Bay. For his tireless efforts, he received the less than princely sum of fifty dollars each month. His preaching brought in a harvest of new believers.

Our Congregation Sent To Internment Camps

After Pearl Harbor was attacked in 1942, bewildered church members were forced to grab whatever they could carry and begin a new life behind barbed wire in desolate inland locations like Rohr, Arkansas, or Manzanar, California. Even though the forces of fear and injustice had scattered them to different internment camps, they found that their faith in Christ was a source of hope and strength. They organized churches wherever they were and kept their eyes on the prize.

A New Identity, A New Name

With the end of World War II, a good portion of the former members began to find their way back to Los Angeles. On April 7, 1946, another young Japanese-American pastor accepted the call to lead this flock. The Spirit used Rev. Paul Nagano mightily to lead many Nisei (second-generation Japanese-Americans) to faith. Even as the members and new converts were struggling to rebuild their personal lives, they each made significant sacrifices in order to rebuild their re-gathered church.

With the burgeoning numbers of English-speaking members, the church was renamed Nisei Baptist Church of Los Angeles and in 1949 the name was changed again, this time to Evergreen Baptist Church of Los Angeles, a reference to its location on the corner of 2nd and Evergreen.

Sometime later, the members voted to form two separate churches, with the Japanese-speaking Issei moving across the street as the "Japanese Baptist Church" and the Nisei and their children remaining as "Evergreen Baptist Church of LA". This must have been an extremely difficult decision, but the Lord used it to set the stage for what God was going to do twenty-five years later. For EBCLA had become something quite unique: a Japanese-American church that only operated in English.

The Impact of The Civil Rights Movement

The 1960's, with the Vietnam War and the Civil Rights Movement, made members of Evergreen-LA wrestle with different issues.

The Rev. Dr. William Shinto led them through some deep soul-searching. The members even questioned the validity of its emphasis on Japanese-Americans as the country at large was in an uproar over racial tensions. God's Spirit used Shinto to expand and enrich the church's understanding of its calling and purpose as an agent of reconciliation and social justice. While other churches were trying to ignore these challenges, EBCLA of the 1960s met them head on.

After Shinto, Rev. Dr. Toru Matsuo briefly led the church. He began to prod the church to establish 'encounter groups,' which were all the rage then, but the leadership didn't feel that this was what God wanted. So Matsuo left and formed the Agape Christian Fellowship in West LA. This became a magnet for many JA and ABC idealistic, 'radical' young-adult Christians, with many of them pooling their assets to purchase an apartment complex where they lived in community. Over time, the influence of ACF among Asian American Christians spread to northern California, even touching parts of the Pacific Northwest and Utah. Sadly, with Matsuo at the helm, ACF eventually came to be seen as a cult. The decision of Evergreen-LA's leaders to oppose his proposal proved to be one that safeguarded the church.

Fire Threatens to Close Evergreen Baptist Church
In 1972, while the Rev. David Hirano was the pastor, a fire nearly destroyed the sanctuary. This could not have come at a worse time; the church was already struggling to survive. After the fire, they had to decide if they should they rebuild, relocate, or shut down. Even though they were few in number, they felt God wanted them to rebuild the ruined sanctuary and keep the ministry alive. Again, through making serious sacrifices, they accomplished both goals.

Thus there was still an Evergreen Baptist Church of LA when Cory Ishida accepted the baton from the beleaguered remnant of about 85 faithful who were there in 1977. Although he lacked a seminary pedigree and had never pastored a church before, the members called him to be their shepherd. Ishida was the first Sansei (third-generation Japanese-American) to pastor the church.

His clearly more-acculturated presence soon attracted growing numbers of ABCs (American Born Chinese) to the church, setting the stage for what was to become a new paradigm for this plucky ministry. In 1981, the church called Ken Fong to be its first full-time associate pastor, thus formally embracing the ABCs in the congregation. Evergreen Baptist Church was now something new: an all-English-speaking Asian-American church.

Leaving Boyle Heights for Rosemead

Pastor Ishida and the members realized by 1983 that the ministry would have to be relocated to the San Gabriel Valley if it was going to reach more Asian-Americans for Christ. Even though they had barely more than 200 members at the time, the church finally bought property in Rosemead and made the move in 1988. The staff and congregation mushroomed over the next ten years, with 1,200 people coming to worship each week. A new paradigm for missions was created and launched, and a new church was planted in the East San Gabriel Valley. Ministries to all ages and stages flourished.

Evergreen Baptist Church of Los Angeles Is Born

By 1996, however, the church seemed to some observers to be in "midlife crisis." Attendance had slipped but was holding steady each week at around 900. There had been some significant turnover of staff. Energy was waning and the vision seemed less clear. That year, Reverend Ishida led the membership to make the daring decision to church plant by "hiving" the existing congregation and staff. Thus, on March 1, 1997, he and his staff left with about 650 people to form Evergreen Baptist Church of San Gabriel Valley (Evergreen-SGV) while Rev. Dr. Ken Fong stayed with the Rosemead campus along with the rest of the congregation which sustained the original charter for the Evergreen Baptist Church of Los Angeles (Evergreen-LA).

Since that historic day, the Lord has seen fit to bless both new congregations. Today, more than a decade and a half later, Evergreen-LA still feels like a new church on the old site: Rev. Dr. Ken Fong is still the senior pastor and, although there are still a handful of staff and leaders from the time of the 'hive,' they've been joined by numerous new ones, and plenty of new people! Now with 8–10 English-speaking Asian Americans and Pacific Islanders as well as a smattering of Euro-, Latino-, and African-Americans, the church has been described as a multi-ethnic church with a pan-Asian American majority. During this time, God's Spirit has sufficiently sharpened and clarified EBCLA's purpose, mission, and vision that the staff and leaders are able to plot a strategic path for the church to become a more reconciled, missional Faith Village, a picture and a preview of what God is doing for all creation.

While this history covered a lot of details, it's worth noting how both Evergreen churches have been fruitful over the years by planting a number of other churches, including Epic Church in Fullerton, California, Lifesong Community Church in Chino, California, and Seeds of Life Church in Alhambra, California.

The second church history features Bay Area Chinese Bible Church, a 60 year-old church in Northern California. When I visited Bay Area Chinese Bible Church several years ago, I was encouraged to see the church's extra efforts to reach different groups of people by having multiple worship venues at its two locations (at that time), including: traditional Mandarin, contemporary Mandarin, Cantonese, traditional English, contemporary English, youth worship, and several others. I also noticed their pastoral staff and leaders attending the same church conferences I do, indicative of their posture to learn and desire to grow.

Bay Area Chinese Bible Church (BACBC) has a very rich and interesting history in the East Bay side of the San Francisco Bay Area. In the summer of 1956, Pastor Sen and June Wong held a two-week Vacation Bible School in their duplex apartment on East 27th Street in Oakland. There was an average daily attendance of approximately 20 children and adults. That November, the Lord led the Wongs to start a Sunday School class in their home.

On the first Sunday, there were a total of 11 in attendance, including Sen and June Wong. Gradually, more attendees began adding to the small group. Soon, a church service was added, then a Wednesday prayer meeting, Sunday evening service, and the young people's club.

In February of 1957, the church moved to a house on Wakefield Avenue in Oakland, just two blocks away. In the summer of 1958 the dirt beneath the house was excavated and a basement chapel was added. This allowed the church to continue growing. In 1961, with a weekly attendance of 115, the church decided to formally incorporate.

In 1964, another home was purchased and remodeled as a church on Oakland's East 29th Street. By 1968, the church was running around 200 in attendance, but it grew to over 500 by 1979, when it decided to start Chinese Christian Schools in two small apartments next door to the church. Already one of the largest Chinese churches in the Bay Area, BACBC desperately needed additional facilities.

In 1985, the church, with over 600 attendees, and school, with almost 300 students, moved to a leased facilities on Fargo Avenue in San Leandro. Over the next 10 years, the size of the church and school have both increased to over 1000 attendees at the church, and almost 900 students at the school. Through the years, the church has had strong youth ministries with an emphasis on Bible teaching. In recent years, the church has grown in its outreach to the Cantonese, Mandarin speaking communities and senior citizens.

In September 2003, the church and school opened a 30,000 square foot educational building in Harbor Bay area of Alameda. In June 2011, when the new 30,000 square foot church worship center had completed, the Alameda site now serves as the main site for the church and school.

In July 2015, we formally closed San Leandro's 750 Fargo Avenue campus after 30 years of church and school ministry at that facility. Our Sunday San Leandro worship venue has moved to James Madison Elementary School, in San Leandro, continuing with English and Cantonese worship services as well as Sunday School Classes.

After 60 years from its first days, the Bay Area Chinese Bible Church seeks to reproduce itself by starting "daughter churches" and training up leaders to staff those new ministries. Families still play a central role but the church also bridges many cultural, social, economic, and geographic barriers. The concept of smaller, localized congregations is consistent with the Chinese culture's emphasis on family and community.

The third church history comes from Quest Church in Seattle, Washington.

After three years of helping plant a church in the suburbs of Seattle (Lynnwood), Pastor Eugene and Minhee felt called to leave the suburbs and to shift from a homogenous (Asian) context to a multiethnic community. After several months in transition, they had their first gathering (7 people) in their living room. Soon thereafter, they began to lead a Bible study in the University District. As the group grew, the gathering shifted from a Bible study to a Sunday worship gathering. In June 2001, they moved locations to the Interbay/Ballard area and used the facility at Interbay Covenant Church. It was during this time that conversations of joining the Evangelical Covenant Church (ECC) became more deliberate. Within a few months, the church (then about 30 people) joyfully began its relationship with the ECC. On October 14, 2001, Quest Church was officially launched.

For the next six years, Quest continued to meet in the Warehouse (now the Q Cafe) on the Interbay Covenant Church campus. After lots of conversations, prayers, and dialogue, Interbay Covenant Church "gave itself" to Quest and "merged" into our community and ministry on June 2, 2007.

Interbay has an amazing history of over 70 years. They built the current church facilities in 1965 and purchased the Warehouse in 1975. More important than the assets Interbay gifted to Quest, they brought a dynamic, beautiful community ready to join Quest and continue the journey as a new community together.

God has continued to work in and through Quest for the last 14 years. Because of our growth blessings we searched for a new church location for several years. After much prayer and discernment, our church membership voted to move forward with the purchase of a new building in the Ballard area. On September 13, 2015 we had our first worship service in our new location.

Through it all, we remain committed to continuing to journey together for the sake of the Gospel.

In this third church history, the humility of the older church willing to give itself and its building to a younger church is admirable and noteworthy. This was extremely difficult, and by no means an easy decision, as detailed in a *Facts & Trends* article, "The Quest to Transform a Church."

When these two churches joined as one, it instantly became multi-generational and much more diverse ethnically. It is a good thing when one generation can pass on the same faith to the next generation. Psalm 145:4 says, "One generation shall commend your works to another, and shall declare your mighty acts."

CHAPTER 10
RAISING UP NEXT GENERATION LEADERS

What kind of future would you like to see for the next generation of Asian Americans? We have a vital role in raising up the next generation of pastors and church leaders. It does not happen by accident and it doesn't happen by prayer alone.

Many Asian immigrants come to America with great hopes for better opportunities and aspirations to the American dream. This was my parents' immigration story. My father brought our young family to America from Taiwan in 1974. I was eight year old and my two younger brothers were six and one. We grew up in rural Virginia, the city of Winchester, with a population of 20,000. My parents upheld a high value for education. They wanted us to study hard and get the best grades in school, believing it was the best path for success in life.

PARENTS MAKE THE BIGGEST DIFFERENCE

Parents make the biggest difference. It's not just the church's leadership that makes it last for more than one generation. Of course, ultimately it's in the sovereignty of God and how people respond to His leading. However, the church can be instrumental in cultivating an environment where parents live out their faith in a loving and affirming manner.

Vern Bengtson examined the religious beliefs and practices of more than 3,500 grandparents, parents, grandchildren, and great-grandchildren over four decades and published his research in a book titled "Families and Faith: How Religion is Passed Down across Generations." In a 2013 Christian Today article interview with Vern Bengtson, two factors stood out in explaining why some parents were successful in passing on their faith:[59]

> #1 "... parents who provide consistent modeling. If the parents aren't consistent, the kids won't have religious role models to emulate."

> #2 "... the quality of the relationship between the child and the parent affects the success or lack of success in transmission. Warm, affirming parents, especially fathers, tend to be the most successful."

The Bible has much to say about how the older generation can pass down their faith to the next generation. It's anchored in the passage known as the "Shema," a Hebrew word for "hear," in Jewish tradition that has been a daily prayer for devout Jews from generation to generation. As it is written in Deuteronomy 6:4-9,

> Hear, O Israel: The Lord our God, the Lord is one. You shall love the Lord your God with all your heart and with all your soul and with all your might. And these words that I command you today shall be on your heart. You shall teach them diligently to your children, and shall talk of them when you sit in your house, and when you walk by the way, and when you lie down, and when you rise. You shall bind them as a sign on your hand, and they shall be as frontlets between your eyes. You shall write them on the doorposts of your house and on your gates.

For one's faith to be alive and active, it has to be more than praying regularly, preserving traditions, and practicing rituals. Faith has to be evident in our relationships—how we love one another. It has to guide us in our discernment to best use the gifts and talents God gave us.

GOD GIFTS EVERYONE DIFFERENTLY

Many Asian American families follow this common narrative: the parents sacrifice greatly to make ends meet, sending their children to the best schools to get the best education, so they can become doctors, lawyers, and engineers in order to gain social status, bring honor to the family name, and provide financial stability. This Asian American narrative is pretty much the same for Christian and non-Christian families alike.

There are two problems with this narrative. First, God doesn't create everyone equal, so not every Asian American should be a doctor, lawyer, or engineer. You're probably familiar with 1 Corinthians 12:4-6 (NIV), "There are different kinds of gifts, but the same Spirit distributes them. There are different kinds of service, but the same Lord. There are different kinds of working, but in all of them and in everyone it is the same God at work." While this passage is speaking of spiritual gifts, the very same God gives different people different natural gifts too. He created people to be teachers, salespersons, programmers, professors, business executives, managers, musicians, artists, dancers, social workers, pastors, missionaries, carpenters, plumbers, and many other kinds of workers.

I followed that narrative myself, as the dutiful eldest son of my family. I did well in math and science during high school, attended college and majored in electrical engineering. After graduating from Virginia Tech, I worked two years as an engineer in Southern Maryland. Then God introduced me to a special, Christian gentleman who changed my life. Buggs Bugnon was a retired Navy senior chief who, in a sense, was my spiritual father. I attended a Bible-teaching church with him and we went through a discipleship program called Operation Timothy. Though we were many years apart in age, had very little in common, he took a sincere interest in me, encouraged me, invested in me, and prayed for me. He shared his life very openly with me, both his victories and his struggles. I spent a lot of time at his home with his very hospitable family. Seeing how he lived out his Christian beliefs beyond just church on Sundays was what sparked my own spiritual awakening.

During the Summer of 1990, one particular Scripture passage kept getting my attention, Matthew 9:36-38 (NIV),

> When he saw the crowds, he had compassion for them, because they were harassed and helpless, like sheep without a shepherd. Then he said to his disciples, "The harvest is plentiful, but the laborers are few; therefore pray earnestly to the Lord of the harvest to send out laborers into his harvest."

I couldn't ignore the fact that this passage kept echoing in my heart as I heard it repeatedly in different settings. These words moved me to action and I received it as a "call to ministry." Seeing how many Asian Americans I went to college with didn't know Christ, I thought that God could use me in some way to reach them—people like me. I thought I should start to prepare for ministry by applying to seminary.

It was with much fear and trepidation for me to respond to this call, because I'm rather timid by nature and I was afraid of what my family would think—I feared being disowned. And I thank God for confirming His calling in 3 ways.

When I told my mentor Buggs about my sense of calling to go to seminary, he was moved emotionally and told me that he'd been praying for a year that God would lead me to seminary, and not just any seminary, specifically Dallas Theological Seminary, which had been an influential seminary for the church I was attending. Secondly, I received encouraging words of confirmation from the pastors at my church. Thirdly, with much prayer support, I approached my non-Christian Dad to tell him of my desire to attend seminary. He responded with permission for me to go. What an answer to prayer!

Oh, and I should mention that being accepted to Dallas Theological Seminary was another confirmation. In January 1991, I packed up all my worldly belongings and drove from Maryland to Dallas.

Not growing up in a Christian family, I went to seminary with the notion that pastoral leadership was all about mastery over the biblical text. So I enrolled for the Master of Theology degree that required learning the Greek and Hebrew languages in which the Bible was originally written in.

However, when I entered into pastoral ministry upon graduating from seminary, the questions people asked had very little to do with Greek or Hebrew. Most congregants I served had everyday concerns about how to know the will of God, what to do with broken relationships, and looking for God's strength and encouragement for life's daily challenges. I believe seminary training gave me a solid biblical foundation and framework for understanding God's desires for humanity, but I had much more to learn if I wanted to be truly effective in my ministry.

HOW FAST THE WORLD CHANGES

Second problem with the Asian American narrative: The world has changed dramatically in the past decade due to digital technologies, social media, and the internet; but the narrative of the Asian American dream has not changed. Just a few years ago, popular YouTube star Freddie Wong was interviewed on the Jimmy Kimmel show.[60] Freddie described how his parents had hoped he would be a doctor or lawyer; and they weren't exactly thrilled that Freddie aspired to be a filmmaker. Surprisingly, things haven't changed since I went to college over 25 years ago.

Education is valuable but no longer enough. Having a college degree may be foundational, but having productive work experiences is much more valuable. The most recent finding on job search is that a resume with education is not as useful as a list of projects with results accomplished. The number of full-time lifelong careers are shrinking. More jobs are requiring the self-awareness of knowing one's transferrable skills and building on developing skills and experiences based on strengths. According to the U.S. Department of Labor's Bureau of Labor Statistics, an average person held more than 11 jobs in a lifetime. And the numbers seem to be trending higher for the next generation, not just the total number of jobs but number of careers as well.[61]

The church has also changed dramatically since the late 90s when I graduated from seminary. Being an effective pastor in today's world requires so much more than knowing and understanding the biblical text. In a world where people have all of the world's information at their fingertips (and easily called up by asking Siri or Alexa), the pastor's role is not only a shepherd who cares and guides, but doing so in the context of today's fast-changing world. Psalm 78:72 describes what's required of a good shepherd—skillfulness: "And David shepherded them with integrity of heart; with skillful hands he led them."

Churches need pastors who can lead with integrity of heart and skill of hand. An effective pastor must have both character (integrity of heart) and competency (skillful hands). In recent years, I've started to notice that young leaders possess much more knowledge than I did when I was their age. They seem more capable and confident. My concern for these young leaders is if they have enough time with mentoring relationships to develop the characters needed for effective ministry to last for a lifetime.

As we read earlier in Matthew 9:38, "The harvest is plentiful, but the laborers are few; therefore pray earnestly to the Lord of the harvest to send out laborers into his harvest." Korean Christians have a great tradition of early morning prayers and prayer mountains where many fervently cry out to God with earnest petitions for their daily needs. But what about other things that need to be prayed for? Asking God to send out more laborers for His ministry? To make our children's spiritual foundation a higher priority than educational achievements? For increasing faith to take bolder steps of faith in raising up more pastors and church leaders for the next generation? Prayer without action is truncated just as faith without works is dead.

MAKING SENSE OF LEADERSHIP

I don't consider myself a natural-born leader, having never aspired to be a class president or taking any leadership role in my school years. Yet I've found myself working in this realm of leadership development for almost 20 years now, more as a strategic advisor training leaders within an organization. I like to describe my contribution as connecting people to people and people to resources. Perhaps that gives me a perspective of seeing the ingredients of leadership more explicitly than someone who has the gift of leadership innately or intuitively.

What is leadership? It's a common question encountered by churches in both Asian and American contexts. For one, leadership is challenging because there are so many different definitions. I recall one speaker say that there are over 6,000 definitions of leadership and tens of thousands of books on leadership. There's certainly a lot of interest in the topic of leadership in the Christian church realm, as indicated by annual conferences such as Catalyst and Willow Creek Association's Global Leadership Summit, both have seen attendance over 30,000.

And then there are pithy sayings that obscure the complexity and multi-faceted dimensions of leadership: "Leadership is influence—nothing more, nothing less." (John Maxwell) "The only definition of a leader is someone who has followers." (Peter Drucker) "Leadership is the capacity to translate vision into reality." (Warren Bennis) "A leader is a person who influences people to accomplish a purpose." (Howard Hendricks) These definitions are useful as a good starting point, but there's so much more to developing a leader.

Reading leadership books, listening to podcasts, enrolling in classes, and going to conferences can be helpful to one's leadership development. When I looked into programs for leadership development, I found basically five types: courses, conferences, cohorts, coaching, and residency. All of these programs can increase one's knowledge of leadership principles and practices. Some programs are better than others at developing leadership competencies and skills. For more details, see this comparison chart of different leadership development programs at multiasian.church/comparison. There's a great deal of content which can be learned through leadership programs, but content alone doesn't make for a skilled leader.

What I found elusive is a coherent way of pulling together all the different aspects of leadership. I suppose that's what makes leadership so dynamic and challenging. Every organization, every group of people, every situation, and every leader is different. Leadership is not like a recipe with instructions to follow and in return, can produce a delicious dish.

First and foremost, leadership does not begin with seeing if you're a leader by having followers. Leadership begins with leading oneself. Self-leadership is the most essential ingredient that cannot be ignored; that's why self-control is listed as a fruit of the spirit in Galatians 5:22-23. Dr. Benjamin Shin said it this way, "If you can't lead yourself, you have no business leading others."

Secondly, leadership has to be learned first-hand through actually leading in real situations with real people. Additionally, we learn to lead by practicing in both the science and the art of leadership principles. The ideal scenario for growing as a leader is to have someone older and wiser who can guide and coach in the same context. This may not be easy to find, particularly in an Asian American ministry.

WHAT NEXT GENERATION LEADERS NEED

In my on-going conversations with younger Asian American leaders and pastors, the number one thing I hear them expressing is wanting to have mentors and role models. That was the need 20 years ago and it is still the need today. But where will they find them?

Sometimes, an older pastor may not know how to mentor because they haven't been mentored themselves, or they refrain from being a mentor because they don't understand the culture and thinking of next generation Asian Americans. Plus, ministering in an Asian American context may be so demanding that it's hard to find time and energy for mentoring.

Some of us Asian Americans may be reluctant to draw attention to our expertise and experiences out of sincere humility. I remember a time when I heard an accomplished Asian American ministry leader share how he was reluctant to call himself a mentor since it might seem presumptuous or boastful. He didn't feel ready because he was too aware of his own shortcomings.

Incidentally, I will not be making the distinction here between mentoring, training, coaching, and leadership development, though there are technical differences for each term. I simply want to highlight the importance of mentoring, and emphasize that it is something we all can do now. I have found this quote from Seth Godin most helpful: "Mentoring is rarely about the facts of the deal (the facts are easily found), but instead is a transfer of emotion and confidence."[62]

I've also observed that many Asian Americans don't think of themselves as leaders, nor do they aspire to be; hence they are unresponsive to leadership development opportunities. Part of that may come from recognizing the weighty responsibility of a leader and the commitment called for. True, it's not a decision to be made lightly. But, again, our world is in desperate need of godly leaders in the church, in the marketplace, and in our government. If Asian Americans with good characters don't step into leadership opportunities to serve people well, those with lesser characters and impure motives won't hesitate to fill the void.

There could be many other reasons why we don't have enough Asian American leaders in the church today. The tendency is to wait and gradually make the effort at diagnosing the issues through research. But that will not get us more leaders now. Working on the solutions imminently to actually develop leaders is what will result in producing more leaders.

For a more thorough exploration on the development of Asian American leaders, I recommend Paul Tokunaga's book, *Invitation to Lead: Guidance for Emerging Asian American Leaders.*[63]

HOW TO RAISE UP NEXT GENERATION LEADERS

What can churches do to raise up the next generation of Asian American pastors and church leaders? I believe there's a lot that older leaders can do, both first generation Asian immigrant as well as non-Asian pastors. Something very powerful happens to a young Asian American when someone older takes time to invest in his or her leadership development. It is a tremendous blessing. Here are three tips to get started:

Prayer: It starts with prayer in asking God for the courage to take steps of faith, because leadership is much more than managing people and running programs. It is also acting in faith with full dependence on God to turn vision into reality. And like Jesus did, pray for discernment to identify and invite the right people to invest time and energy in the development of leaders.

Preparation: Start with basic training. You don't have to be a leadership expert to help a younger leader. You can meet weekly with young leaders by simply reading a leadership book and discuss it together. Conferences are also valuable for training as a shared experience. This website oases. church has the largest database of Christian conferences for you to find one based on topic, location, and dates. Never go to a conference alone; it's so much more valuable when you attend with others. Shared experiences can strengthen relationships in the long run.

Practice: You don't have to design an entire curriculum and program to train up leaders. When you go through everyday activities of being a leader, use them to be learning opportunities. My favorite book on leadership development is *Exponential: How You and Your Friends Can Start a Missional Church Movement* by Dave and Jon Ferguson. This book has many great examples and a profoundly simple basic steps for developing leadership skills:

1. I do. You watch. We talk.
2. I do. You help. We talk.
3. You do. I help. We talk.
4. You do. I watch. We talk.
5. You do. Someone else watches.

Here's another useful chart that helps to visualize these basic steps for leadership development from Daniel Im's blog:[64]

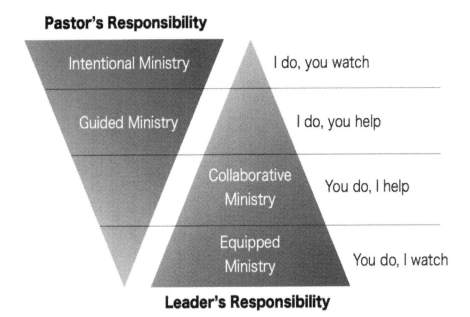

We have many great leadership resources available to us. Maybe it's the over-abundance that is paralyzing; it may be hard to know where to start when there's so many to choose from. I've compiled a list of recommended books, courses, conferences, and other resources at multiasian.church/leadership. The important thing is to start now. And, in a fast-changing world, leadership is not something you can learn once and be done with it; leaders have to be learners.

THREE MINISTERS WALKED INTO A DINER

On January 30, 2015, three ministers walked into a diner. I know this might sound like a great opening for a joke, but this is actually a true story. The three of us happened to be next generation ministry leaders of Asian American descent: one Korean American, one Vietnamese American, and one Chinese American.

As we were getting to know each other, we discovered our commonalities as bi-cultural Asian Americans, our like-mindedness for developing future church leaders, and what we could be accomplishing together. We believe that Asian American pastors have something valuable and unique to contribute to the church with the very essence of who we are and who God has created us to be in this generation. While each of us has attended many Christian conferences, we recognized that Asian Americans needed our own space. (You can also watch the raw video footage of this back story at thirty.network/backstory.)

A year later, we launched the **Thirty Network** to gather 30 Asian American pastors and church leaders, in their 30s, for 30 hours, to talk about the next 30 years. We started with an invitation-only event to begin forming a relational community with access to mentoring, coaching, and ministry opportunities towards shaping the next 30 years of Asian American Christian leaders in the church, both domestically and internationally.

Even though we had no staff and no budget, we had a vision and God provided through the generosity of volunteers and sponsors. Thirty Network partnered with several mainstream Christian sponsors who believed in what we were starting and wanted to invest in the future of Asian Americans. Our invitation list was compiled by recommendation from credible pastors. As we gathered, we listened to a seasoned church leader from mainstream culture speak on how we can prepare for our next 30 years. We also made time to hear from one another because every participant has something to contribute and we wanted everyone's voice heard.

At the end of the 30 interactive hours, we surveyed all the participants and confirmed how valuable this gathering was. All respondents would recommend this gathering to a friend. The high value was noted in comments like, "Valued spending time and fellowshipping with other pastors and workers," "Brainstorming sessions and ideas from others," and "Networking, being encouraged, stimulating conversations." This was a proof-of-concept, or beta test.

We shared the vision of Thirty Network with key leaders in cities like New York City, Los Angeles, Chicago, Houston, and Philadelphia. It has been received enthusiastically. Our volunteer core team is willing and able to convene a gathering when four ingredients come together: A speaker (to provide wise mentoring), a sponsor (to help with financial costs), a space (where we can gather for 30 hours of interactive conversations), and a squad (to invite the right people).

We are building this plane as it flies, as the saying goes. In addition to the signature event of a 30-hour intensive, Thirty Network is also launching open-access gatherings as a conference add-on because having face-to-face interaction together is irreplaceably valuable. Thirty Network's next gathering is in October 2016 as a pre-conference session at the Exponential West 2016 church leadership conference. After we've had our group session, we will join the larger conference together.

Thirty Network is doing its part, a small part, to advancing Asian American pastors and church leaders for multiethnic churches in multicultural America and to the ends of the earth. Upon completion of authoring this book, I've been inspired to do one more thing for Thirty Network: 100% of the proceeds from the sales of this book will go to Thirty Network.

What are you inspired to do?

The future of Asian Americans in a multiethnic world can be significantly shaped by those who have more life experiences. If the older generation of Asian Americans will bless the next generation with what God has gifted them, more people can be reached for Jesus Christ. The next chapter will explore the possible future we can have as Asian Americans.

CHAPTER 11
UNLEASHING OUR POTENTIAL

There's a frequently quoted line from the popular movie Spiderman: "With great power comes great responsibility." This fictional account from a graphic novel, known as a comic book to a previous generation, seems to echo an ancient text with the words of Jesus: "Everyone to whom much was given, of him much will be required, and from him to whom they entrusted much, they will demand the more" (Luke 12:48).

For the Asian American population, currently at 21 million,[65] projected to nearly double by 2050,[66] we have the highest educational attainment and highest median family income of any racial ethnic group in America when statistically aggregated together. This aggregated data does obscure a significant part of the Asian American population who lives below the poverty line and has serious financial and social needs. Disaggregating the data will quickly debunk the "model minority" myth.

However, if the aggregated data shows the overall achievement of Asian Americans on the whole, what does the disaggregated data say about the overall achievements of those Asian Americans who really are among those with the most education and the most income? Since there are Asian Americans among the poorest, this also means there are Asian Americans among the richest.

What does God require from these Asian Americans that are the smartest and richest? What does God require from those that are the blessed with the most resources? There is so much more that God can do through highly-resourced Asian Americans who are sold out as followers of Christ and desire to be strategically generous with their vast resources. Our responsibility is to respond with our abilities so that we can experience even greater joy of God's blessings. Would that Jesus' words be true: "it is more blessed to give than to receive" (Acts 20:35).

Allow me to share three of the most strategic ways that Asian American Christians can do together to make the greatest impact for the Kingdom of God.

HOW VOICES INFLUENCE

First, Asian American Christians can use our voices in the online public square.

In this internet age, communication is democratized and available for anyone to speak to the world in an instant. The social media world enables us to have a public voice. In 2002, a homeless guy in Nashville could blog by going to the public library and using a computer terminal.[67] Kevin Barbieux has continued blogging online[68] and using his voice as an advocate for the homeless.

In 2011, citizens used social media to coordinate the communications of their protests which overturned governments in Tunisia, Egypt, Libya, and Yemen, in what is now known as "Arab Spring." If social media could be used in such powerful ways as to overturn governments, what are we, the church, doing with it to serve God?

Millions of people use search engines everyday to search for things of interest and to find answers to questions. What do people find when they search for Asian Americans? Here's a quick snapshot of Asian American culture in the public square: there are Asian American stars on YouTube with their entertaining videos of music and comedy. There are two broadcast television shows, Fresh Off the Boat and Dr. Ken. There's a pop culture commentary blog by "Angry Asian Man."

But what do people find when they search for perspectives from Asian American Christians? In chapter 3, I listed reports that show the significant size of Asian American Christianity. Those numbers represent a lot of voices.

However, when searching online for Asian American Christian views regarding world issues today, they are difficult to find. If we remain silent, we remain invisible. If we're invisible, our influence is diminished. In a world immersed in digital communications everywhere, how can we better proclaim the Good News and engage in current events with our unique perspectives as Asian American followers of Christ?

Making a difference means using our voices to influence—communicating through audio messages and through written words. In a previous generation, we had television, radio, and books. Today, we have web videos, podcasts, ebooks, and blogs.

Don't limit sharing your valuable insights to only people you meet in person—where it is communicated once and lost forever. Other people can benefit too if you utilize the online channels available, where your words can have both a longer shelf life and much farther reach.

In other words, the internet empowers us to share our message to influence people far and wide. We have personal devices readily within reach to share the message, whether instantly through livestreaming, or recorded. We are producing content all the time, and it takes just a little extra effort to share it with the world and exponentially increase our influence.

We don't need to have an extensive media production to share our message. We can start now and improve over time. When we form the habit of using our voices in the online world, we'll receive feedback from others that can help us improve our communication skills.

For instance, Julie Powell started a blog in 2002 to document her learning experience in cooking through the recipes of Julia Child. That became a Hollywood movie *Julie & Julia* in 2009. Michael Hyatt started blogging in 2004 on the topic of leadership and captured the lessons he learned along the way that he compiled into a best-selling book titled, *Platform: Get Noticed in a Noisy World*, published in 2012. I started blogging in 1999, and the many years of regular blogging have helped me develop my skills to write this book.

Here's my best tip on how to get started. If you like to write, start a blog (at wordpress.com). If you like to talk, start a podcast (at spreaker.com). If you like to talk with your hands, make a video (at youtube.com). What's made social media so powerful and widely used is because it is relatively easy to use and quick to learn. Start using your voice online to influence the world for good. Yoda, in *Star Wars*, offered sagely advice: "Do. Or do not. There is no try."

Here's another thought: if you happened to be technically-challenged, ask someone younger to help. Make this an opportunity for reverse mentoring.

We need your words, the messages from the good guys, to fill the online world with beauty, goodness, and truth to displace all the negative noises that are out there. In the beginning, God created the heaven and the earth. God spoke and it came into existence: the light, the night, the seas, the fishes, the birds, the animals. We are made in His image. Just as His words are powerful to create a new world, so can our words change the world.

I would love to know about your online presence and how you're using your voice to make a difference in the world. Please share your web address with me at multiasian.church/contact and I'll compile a list to raise our collective voices together.

HOW IMPACT MULTIPLIES

The movement that abolished the slave trade in the British Empire, culminating with the Slavery Abolition Act in 1833, was led by William Wilberforce. This incredible societal change was not accomplished alone. Wilberforce was part of a small group which came to be known as the

Clapham Sect, "a network of friends and families in England, with William Wilberforce as its centre of gravity, who were powerfully bound together by their shared moral and spiritual values, by their religious mission and social activism, by their love for each other, and by marriage."[69]

This is just one example that illustrates how impact multiples when a small group of key leaders work together towards a vision bigger than anyone of them could possibly achieve alone. As I looked for what changes the trajectory of human history, I've observed how some of the most powerful impact was accomplished when a small group of key leaders met together regularly to work on a shared vision.

Over 2,000 years ago, a small group of disciples chosen by Jesus Christ impacted the world in so many ways. They inspired the creation of institutions like hospitals, schools, universities, and churches with over a billion followers of Christianity.

In present day, there are highly-strategic gatherings like the Aspen Ideas Festival,[70] World Economic Forum,[71] and Renaissance Weekend,[72] which convene key leaders together regularly, to build relationships, learn, and to have conversations for greater social impact.

A small conference called TED, an acronym for technology, entertainment, and design launched in 1984.[73] This conference met annually from 1990 to 2001 to feature presentations on the latest innovations by experts in those fields. TED's vision was expanded in 2009 by Chris Anderson into an elite gathering that presented world-changing ideas under the slogan, "Ideas Worth Spreading." Despite the fact that the enormous price tag for a TED conference registration makes it only affordable to a self-selected attendance of movers and shakers, the conference presentations, known as TED talks, are recorded as videos and posted online for free, so these potentially world-changing ideas can spread at ted.com and on YouTube to reach the masses everyday.

Where did Anderson, a powerful curator of world-changing ideas, get his zeal for changing the world? Perhaps it is no coincidence that he was born the son of British medical missionaries and grew up in Afghanistan, India and Pakistan.[74]

In 2007, Gabe Lyons launched the Q conference with a vision for Christian leaders to renew and restore culture. In its early years as an annual conference, Q has spawned local and regional events to facilitate relationships and conversations. Since it gathers influencers and aspires to influence society for the common good, in other words, to change the world, Q has drawn comparison as the "Christian TED Talks."[75]

When I look upon our tribe of Asian American Christians, there are good networks on the local level and certain regional areas. What I have yet seen is an annual summit that convenes key leaders among Asian American Christians across America, to kickstart the conversations around a shared agenda as the Body of Christ. I find myself looking at the landscape from a different perspective, a national one.

Over the years, I have heard many reasons—historically, culturally, geographically, and financially—for why it is so hard to build a coalition of Asian American Christian leaders across these fruited plains. These reasons are contributing factors that make it challenging to convene. Yet I believe we have the supernatural power of God to overcome challenges like these. Furthermore, Asian Americans have some of the most educated and resourced people whom God has gifted to make this happen.

I believe that the absence of this kind of annual national gatherings hinders our development on the whole. We stay stagnant, isolated in our struggles, while "reinventing the wheel" trying to solve the same old problems.

Could it be that because this is so challenging, it could potentially have the most valuable and lasting impact if accomplished?

Does this sound like a compelling vision to you? It's certainly worth a conversation. I'm praying for God to bring the right people together to seek first the Kingdom of God for our tribe. Pray with me in creating a greater future for Asian Americans in a multiethnic world.

HOW IDEAS BECOME REALITY

For an idea to become reality, a project to be completed, or an organization to be sustainable, it takes resources, specifically, financial resources. When people work to earn money, that money is exchanged for food and other goods used for daily necessities. Sometimes accumulating wealth through salary, sales, or investments can result in more money than required for basic needs. This excess wealth can be saved for a rainy day or for retirement. But what if we're blessed with more financial resources than we could possibly use in our lifetime? It should be recognized that a person's abilities and opportunities to becoming wealthy ultimately comes from God, and it is to God whom we respond with our abilities, in this case, with our extra financial abilities.

Since the overall numbers show that Asian Americans have the highest family median income, and we also know that the disaggregated numbers indicate a significant portion of Asian Americans live at or below the poverty level, the corollary implies that there are Asian Americans who are very wealthy. A small percentage of people have attained a status known as financially independent or independently wealthy—having more than enough saved up to cover a lifetime of expenses. This means working to earn a living is essentially optional. What an interesting concept for a few. This opens up a whole realm of opportunities along with a lot of responsibilities.

The foresight of the founding fathers in America recognized the potential of the wealthy to do good in society, and setup a favorable infrastructure to incentivize charity voluntarily. That philosophy of government has made it the role of nonprofit organizations to develop programs to serve the community's needs rather than having an excessive amount of government programs.

The concept of charitable tax deductions is a notable incentive to encourage people to be generous and charitable by giving cash donations in exchange for a lower federal income tax. From a Christian perspective, it is smart stewardship in maximizing how far money can go to do more good.

What has made American society flourish are the generous gifts of public philanthropy, not government programs, from the likes of Henry Ford, Andrew Carnegie, W. K. Kellogg, John Templeton, J. Howard Pew, Bill & Melinda Gates, and numerous others.[76] Most relevantly, the latest research about Asian Americans mentioned in this book was made possible by the Pew Charitable Trust, funded by the excess wealth of J. Howard Pew.

Public philanthropy serves as a positive role model for generosity and heightens awareness for community needs so that more people can benefit as well as contribute. With Asian cultural values influencing many Asian Americans, generosity in philanthropy tends to be done quietly and privately.

But human nature being what it is, private philanthropy or anonymous giving, does not add positive encouragement for others to give more or to be generous. There's a greater good that can benefit many more when role models for public philanthropy encourage in a multiplier effect. Though cynics may be suspicious of the motives behind someone else's generosity, the positive results from generosity demonstratively overshadow the impure motives of a few.[77]

So what would it look like to have role models for philanthropy by Asian American Christians? In the secular world, generous Asian Americans have formed nonprofit organizations such as Asian Americans/Pacific Islanders in Philanthropy. In American Christianity, there's an annual conference called The Gathering[78] where generous Christian donors share and learn from each other about strategic philanthropy and expanding their vision in giving joyfully.

There is not yet a counterpart for followers of Christ in our Asian American tribe that convenes as a community of strategic philanthropy. Can you imagine what a community like this can do if we open the floodgates of generosity from Asian American Christians? It will overflow into even greater impact for our nation and the world. This community can be the catalyst to start conversations about Asian American Christian philanthropy, and create role models for generosity through setting the example.

For churches and pastors of all ethnic backgrounds, the subject of money is uncomfortable to talk about. But there are particular challenges in talking about money in Asian and Asian American contexts, as illustrated in this excerpt of an interview with a church leader in China named Raymond:

> This is what he found through interacting with basic-level pastors: when pastors talk about money, they feel difficult, and shy.

At the beginning, he thought that was strange, later he found that basic-level pastors really had difficulties to open their mouths and ask followers to give money; he also found it had to do with the Chinese culture: it is hard to talk about money frankly.

He thinks basic-level pastors need to have the courage to frankly talk about the truth on giving, need to correctly educate their disciples on the truth of one tenth giving. The Bible talked about money and sacrifice openly, and pastors need to face sacrifice and fund raising correctly, and to educate and execute appropriately, otherwise it is very hard to develop churches.

The Chinese Churches have comparatively more conservative theological traditions, and formed an idea "the poorer, the more spiritual"; people should serve without pay and that is believed to be the demonstration of "living with faith."

For this, Raymond believes, if we can face sacrifice and fund raising in the right manner, we can develop churches and services much better. A lot of pastors can then serve God full time, instead of working for others to earn a living, while doing a lot of service.[79]

Jesus Christ talked often about money. 15% of everything Jesus ever taught was on the topic of money and possessions—more than His teachings on heaven and hell combined.[80] 16 of the 38 parables were concerned with how to handle money and possessions. In the Gospels, an amazing one out of ten verses (288 in all) deal directly with the subject of money.[81] it should follow that pastors would talk about money to their flocks too.

My friend and colleague Chris Willard said it well, "Being generous is being Godly." We would do well to make a more explicit and tighter connection between money and spirituality. I'd suggest digging into the book he co-authored with Jim Sheppard, Contagious Generosity: Contagious Generosity: Creating a Culture of Giving in Your Church.

Knowing how to manage wealth and being generous is a vital part of being godly and Christ-like. The better indicator of Christian maturity is generosity with time, talents, and treasures, rather than merely religious devotion and Bible knowledge. "For where your treasure is, there your heart will be also" (Matthew 6:21). Churches and pastors must teach biblically about money and wealth because Christian maturity can't take place without it.

We can celebrate and rejoice with Asian Americans whom God has already inspired to be extremely generous in philanthropy. Their actions are inspirations to us all.

The largest single donation in the history of Biola University was a $12 million gift[82] from Alton Lim, a Chinese American immigrant who gave generously as an expression of thanksgiving for God's guidance and provision throughout his life. This gift also aligns with two areas of passion for Alton Lim and his family: Scripture and science. One of Alton Lim's four children, Daniel, explained: "God has blessed him financially, and he wanted to find a tangible means to return back to God what is originally His. He acknowledges the fact that ... every penny he's ever had in his pocket belongs to God. As he puts it, in his later years now, he wants to be able to do something tangible to express that."

Good philanthropy is already fueling scholarships, academic education, and research on health and technology. There are more opportunities yet to be explored. What if high net-worth followers of Christ strategically invested in long-term gains for God's Kingdom, things that may not be measurable in quarterly or annual reports? We have the agility to experiment with trial and error, to capture lessons learned and to share them freely. As I write this, I've just heard a speaker's exhortation that money is not the problem; we need the vision to dream bigger.

IMAGINING THE FUTURE

Yes, it may seem crazy and risky of me to open up my playbook for all to see. I've heard some say that ideas should incubate privately and not be so openly shared. Some might even steal my ideas. But I sincerely believe that more good things can happen if we don't care who gets the credit. If any of these ideas are inspired by God and can be adapted or refined to be something more effective, then by all means, share. All glory be unto our generous God.

Would you like more? I've written more on the topic of our future in this article, "Brighter Future for American Evangelical Church."[83] I humbly submit before you as seeds of inspiration, my prayer for Asian Americans to join in on what God's doing in today's generation. And, Lord willing, I'll continue blogging on this topic at djchuang.com.

CHAPTER 12
CLOSING THOUGHTS

I'm extremely hopeful for the future of Asian Americans in our multiethnic world. My prayer is that this book would be an inflection point for a new beginning.

In an open letter from James Choung (who was the National Director of Asian American Ministries at InterVarsity/USA in 2012) published in INHERITANCE Magazine, he quoted a prediction from two historians about the tremendous potential for Asian Americans:

> Historians William Strauss and Neil Howe studied American generations as far back as 1584. Based on their findings, they took some guesses at what future generations would look like. ... In their book Generations, they predicted that Asian Americans would be "a major cultural and intellectual force" by 2025–like the German descendants in the 1880s and 1890s, and their Jewish counterparts of the 1930s and 1940s.[84]

For the record, here's the exact wording from the book *Generations*: "Midlife Asian-Americans will establish their ethnic group as a major cultural and intellectual force, akin to the midlife German Gilded or midlife Jewish Lost."[85]

That quote prompted a shift in my own thinking. For too long, being bicultural had been perceived (and reinforced by some) as a liability because it felt like not fitting in anywhere and having no sense of belonging. But that perception doesn't have to define reality or limit our future. We can reframe that. I now believe being Asian American is more, not less, than being either Asian only or American only. In a fast-changing world that we find ourselves in, with global travel and increasingly accelerating connectivity via mobile and social, being bicultural means a built-in agility to adapt into more contexts than someone with only a monocultural experience. Perhaps as the historians are anticipating, Asian Americans will make a great contribution in the near future.[86]

I recently became an empty-nester when my one and only son graduated from high school and started college. When my son received his diploma at the commencement ceremony, that moment marked a new beginning and a transition for him and for myself. It gave me more discretionary time to work on this book project.

It also heightened my concern for the many Asian American teens who are making that transition from high school into college. For teens who grew up in ethnic Asian churches, such transition is often marked with leaving the ethnic Asian church or the Christian faith altogether, dubbed with the moniker, "silent exodus." But to be fair, an alarming rate of non-Asian teens in American churches also leave their faith behind when they leave for college. Different researches have estimated the youth-to-college attrition rate as high as 61% to 88%.[87]

At the same time in recent years, there's been a significant response to the Gospel among next generation Asian American college students. A 2006 *Christianity Today* article observed this trend: "Asian students are more likely to show Christian commitment than other ethnic groups, including whites."[88] Asian Americans comprise a large part of Christian fellowships at college campuses like UC Berkeley, Harvard, MIT, Stanford, Princeton, and Yale.[89]

InterVarsity/USA and InterVarsity Christian Fellowship of Canada co-host the Urbana student missions conference for college students once every three years with an average estimate of 16,000 conference goers. Urbana has seen a steady growth of Asians and Asian Americans in attendance, from 24.4% in 2009, 39% in 2012, to 40% in 2015. As this book is being written, InterVarsity Christian Fellowship/USA elected and installed its first Asian American president, Tom Lin, in August 2016.

Many Asian Americans have a formative experience which shapes our Christian lives through contextualized campus ministries like InterVarsity, Epic Movement (an Asian American ministry of Cru, formerly known as Campus Crusade for Christ), and Asian American Christian Fellowship. But after college, students re-enter society as young adults, start their careers and build families. This second transition is also a challenging one. Asian American college graduates tend to have a difficult time finding a church home to replicates the same level of energy and enthusiasm that they've experienced during their college years. That's quite a spiritual letdown. While the first transition from high school to college has received attention as a phenomena dubbed "silent exodus," this second transition is also very critical.

Asian American college graduates are less likely to return to the ethnic Asian church, though a small percentage may return when they get married and have children, seeking the best opportunity to reconnect with their Asian heritage and culture. Some choose to attend larger majority-culture churches, and there's nothing wrong with that. But a larger percentage of Asian American college graduates will most likely disengage from their Christian faith all together, and be numbered among the "dones" and "nones."

These are the two most critical transitions we should pay attention to in multi-Asian churches in hopes that we can collectively create a seamless pathway through all the stages of life by having a better handoff from high school to college, and from college back to the church. If we don't work on making these transitions smoother, we are making our ministry to the next generation harder than it needs to be. In this sense, evangelism is harder than discipleship.

Part of the solution will be the multi-Asian churches as I've written about in this book.

Part of the solution will emerge from Asian American pastors receiving theological training at renowned seminaries like Talbot School of

Theology (enrollment is 32% Asian American/ Pacific Islander), Westminster Theological Seminary (24%), and Fuller Theological Seminary (10.6%).[90]

Part of the solution have yet to be birthed in the imagination of the next generation as God would call His children and inspire them to accomplish greater things yet to come.

By way of review, Asian Americans are the fastest-growing racial ethnic grouping, and in less than 30 years from now, there will be no racial majority; or to say it another way, whites will no longer be the majority in US by 2043.[91] Currently, the majority of children under the age of one are already non-white.[92] Ed Stetzer noted how American Christianity is not dying (I can hear Ed shouting, "Stop saying the church in America is dying!"). The American church is very much in transition, and one of those transitions may well be the faster growth in the number of Christians among people of color. This has yet to be reflected on the stages and pages of evangelical media.

This may be too early to call a trend, but I'm starting to notice a leading edge of churches intentionally going multi-lingual to better reach more people groups, not as separate language congregations, but developing an intentional cross-cultural Christian community.

This multiethnic diversity in the United States gives evangelical churches a greater potential to better serve the global village if the church will take bigger and bolder steps to engage this diversity. Granted, not every neighborhood in America is overwhelmingly ethnically diverse, but the growth is evident. The nations have already come. They're at our doorsteps!

Let me hit pause here and let the conversations begin. This book is intended to be a conversation starter for church leaders to engage in robust discussions for effective ministry.

I sincerely invite your thoughts, questions, and comments to be posted online at multiasian.church where we can have open conversations to discuss the many topics mentioned in this book.

We can also have a private conversation using any one of the communication channels readily available: email, phone, and social media—see page 139 for my contact info. It's your call and I'm eager to hear from you.

Finally, I will be adding resources and links at multiasian.church as readers contribute and new publications are released. To stay in touch, subscribe to email updates at multiasian.church/subscribe and like the Facebook page at facebook.com/multiasian.church.

The possibilities and the potential for a brighter future are limitless. It is what we make of it. What are you waiting for?

ACKNOWLEDGMENTS

This is the extra space in the book where I can give thanks to all the special people in my life, kind of like how actresses and actors usually start their Oscar acceptance speech with people they want to thank. Yes, this is the space where I am giving myself permission to be bloggy and casual. I think it's more meaningful for people to see their names listed here rather than for me to write an explanation for why they're being acknowledged.

Plus, there's also the fear of missing someone in my remembrance and thinking up of all the people I sincerely wanted to thank, so to those unintentionally omitted, will you accept my apologies and find it in your heart to forgive me? Would an autographed copy of a printed edition of this book be an acceptable peace offering? :)

Thanks to Jesus Christ my Lord, for you alone have the words of life.

Thank you Rachelle and Jeremiah (who helped proofread the book) for bringing great occasions of joy and happiness into my life on a daily basis and indulging my love for churches and sharing in our family tradition of worshipping at as many churches as possible on Christmas and Easter. Life is more than great adventure and glad you're up for it.

Thanks to my Dad and Mom for the loving sacrifices that instilled my life with good values; to my brothers D.C. and Deef for practical kindnesses over the years; to my in-laws, Dr. and Mrs. Woo, thank you for your prayers and the blessings that overflow from a Christian heritage from generation to generation.

Thanks to my editor Diana Sun for plowing through the book's manuscript and again to my dear wife Rachelle for the book design. Thanks to Sam George for the research data of the Asian diaspora. Thanks to Eric Quan for being the most prolific commenter while reading the rough draft of this book posted online.

Thanks to Paul & Alice Chou for your being good role models of faith and generosity, appreciate the years of how you've opened up opportunities that expanded my vision. Thanks to Buggs & Ann Bugnon for your ever-generous hospitality and how you've changed the entire trajectory of my life, for which I am ever grateful.

Thanks for dear friends along my life journey and how you've given me support and strength to thrive: Brent Wong, Paul Wang Jr., Jeff & Rachel Lee, Amos Kwon, David & Lucy Wang, LT & Lauren Tom, Marc Payan, Jon & Yvonne Meader. Thanks to the encouragers that spoke gracious words of wisdom into my life: Ed Choy, John Tung, Rudy Carrasco, David D. Kim, Jeffrey Jue, David Wong, Curtis Lowe, Arnold & Effie Wong, Benjamin Twinamaani, David Hsu, Allen Banez, David Gunn, John Chow, Chu-Chin Ling-Ling Chen, Chris Lagerlof, Tom Kang, Craig Chong, Angela Ferraro, Will Mancini, Stan Endicott.

Thanks to the pastors and people in these churches that served as my spiritual homes and poured into my life during particular seasons of my life: Calvary Baptist Church in Winchester, Virginia, Blacksburg Christian Fellowship in Blacksburg, Virginia, SAYSF Bible Church in Lexington Park, Maryland, Asian American Baptist Church in Richardson, Texas, Ambassador Bible Church in Northern Virginia, Bridgeway Community Church in Columbia, Maryland, Washington International Church in Washington DC, ROCKHARBOR in Costa Mesa, California, and Saddleback Church in Orange County, California.

Thanks to my colleagues and co-laborers who share my joy in discovering and cultivating church innovations (even as it might border on being an obsession with churches) including: Dave Travis, Todd Rhoades, Kenny Jahng, Nils Smith, Jay Kranda, Cynthia Ware, Kent Shaffer, Linda Stanley, Greg Ligon, Keith Young, Brent Dolfo, Geoff & Sherry Surratt, Chris Willard, Jim Sheppard, Eric & Liz Swanson, Dave Ferguson, Todd Wilson, Bob Buford, Mark DeYmaz, Ed Stetzer, Tony Ferraro, Charles Lee, Jonathan Ro. Thanks to the team at Exponential Network—Dave Ferguson, Todd Wilson, Terri Saliba, Bill Couchenour—for inviting us into the family. We stand on the shoulders of those who've prepared the soil and cultivated a nourishing environment for the next generations of Asian American church leaders and pastors. Of course there are too many to name, though I can name some that have touched me personally whom I'm particularly thankful: Ray Chang, Benjamin Shin, Sheryl Silzer, Margaret Yu, Timothy Tseng, Ken Fong, Louis Lee, Peter Cha, Cory Ishida, Joseph Tsang, Kevin Doi, Seth Kim, Charles Lee, Eugene Cho, David Choi, Drew Hyun, Danny Kwon, Daniel Im, David Park, Daniel So, Tommy Dyo, James Choung.

Thanks to each and every one of the pastors that sacrificed and stepped out in faith to plant a next generation multi-Asian church. This book is really about the story of your churches and what God is beginning to do in and through you. May you be continually filled with the Spirit to serve and inspire our next generations as well, both Asian Americans and non-Asians alike.

And thanks to my dream team for launching Thirty Network with me–Kevin Nguyen, Sam Yoon, Angela Yee, and John Shin–may God use us to be a blessing to many more.

Lastly, thank you for reading all the way to the very end of this book. I hope to get to chat with you and perhaps even meet you one day on this side of heaven.

ABOUT THE AUTHOR

DJ Chuang is a strategy consultant, currently working with the .BIBLE Registry, a new top-level domain for all things Bible. He's worked with Christian organizations and ministries like American Bible Society, Worship Leader Magazine, Leadership Network, L^2 Foundation and has clocked in 5 years of pastoral ministry vocationally.

MultiAsian.Church is the first book entirely authored by DJ Chuang. He's also edited 2 previously-published books, *Asian American Youth Ministry* and *Conversations: Asian American Evangelical Theologies in Formation*. He has been blogging at his personal website—djchuang. com—since 1999, curating many links to resources pertaining to churches multiethnic and/or Asian American, eclectically sharing about things that catch his attention, particularly innovative developments in churches, Asian American and multiethnic cultures, internet and social media.

He is a graduate of Dallas Theological Seminary (Th.M. Pastoral Leadership) and Virginia Tech (B.S. Electrical Engineering.) He resides in Orange County, California, with his artistic wife Rachelle and they have one son named Jeremiah. Lastly, DJ's often spotted wearing orange at conferences.

Connect with DJ Chuang
Email: djchuang@multiasian.church
Phone: +1 949-243-7260
Web: djchuang.com
Twitter: @djchuang
Facebook: facebook.com/djchuang

ENDNOTES

1   "Estimated Total of Cable Channels Offered in 2014." FCC Video
         Competition Report & NCTA Estimates. https://www.ncta.com/industry-data

2   "Internet Usage and 2015 Population in North America." Miniwatts
         Marketing Group, May 2016. http://www.internetworldstats.com/stats14.htm

3   "U.S. Census Bureau Projections Show a Slower Growing, Older, More
         Diverse Nation a Half Century from Now." U.S. Census Bureau, December
         12, 2012. https://www.census.gov/newsroom/releases/archives/
         population/cb12-243.html

4   The author has compiled a list of books about multiethnic churches at
         http://djchuang.com/multi.

5   "Weeks Population: Who First Said 'Demography is Destiny'?." 2013.
         http://weekspopulation.blogspot.com/2013/10/who-first-said-
         demography-is-destiny.html

6   "Population Clock." U.S. Census Bureau, 2013. http://www.census.gov/
         popclock/

7   "Annual Estimates of the Resident Population by Sex, Race Alone or
         in Combination, and Hispanic Origin." U.S. Census Bureau, Population
         Division, June 2016. http://factfinder.census.gov/bkmk/table/1.0/en/
         PEP/2015/PEPSR5H?slice=Year~est72015 For the Asian American
         population in this book, I will be referring to the total Asian population
         in the "Race Alone or in Combination" category and not including the
         "Native Hawaiian and Other Pacific Islander" category.

8   "Table 10. Projections of the Population by Sex, Hispanic Origin, and
         Race for the United States: 2015 to 2060 (NP2014-T10)." U.S. Census
         Bureau, Population Division, December 2014. http://www.census.gov/
         population/projections/data/national/2014/summarytables.html

9   "About." U.S. Census Bureau, July 2013. http://www.census.gov/topics/
         population/race/about.html

10   Luke 2:1-5 (ESV)

11   "About." U.S. Census Bureau, July 2013. http://www.census.gov/topics/
         population/race/about.html

12   "Social Justice | Topics | Christianity Today." 2012. http://www.
         christianitytoday.com/ct/topics/s/social-justice/

13   "The Rise of Asian Americans." Washington, DC: Pew Research Center, June 2012. http://www.pewsocialtrends.org/2012/06/19/the-rise-of-asian-americans/

14   "U.S. Census Bureau Projections Show a Slower Growing, Older, More Diverse Nation a Half Century from Now." U.S. Census Bureau, December 12, 2012. https://www.census.gov/newsroom/releases/archives/population/cb12-243.html

15   "America: A Nation on the Move." Random Samplings, the blog of U.S. Census Bureau, December 10, 2012. http://blogs.census.gov/2012/12/10/america-a-nation-on-the-move/

16   Chalabi, Mona. "How Many Times Does The Average Person Move?" FiveThirtyEight, January 29, 2015. http://fivethirtyeight.com/datalab/how-many-times-the-average-person-moves/

17   "Chapter 1: Portrait of Asian Americans" in "The Rise of Asian Americans." Washington DC: Pew Research Center, June 2012. http://www.pewsocialtrends.org/2012/06/19/chapter-1-portrait-of-asian-americans/

18   "Language map: What's the most popular language in your state?" Slate, 2014. http://www.slate.com/articles/arts/culturebox/2014/05/language_map_what_s_the_most_popular_language_in_your_state.html

19   "The Rise of Asian Americans." Washington, DC: Pew Research Center, June 2012. Updated April 2013. http://www.pewsocialtrends.org/2012/06/19/the-rise-of-asian-americans/

20   ibid.

21   ibid.

22   Le, C.N. "The Model Minority Image." Asian-Nation. 2003. http://asian-nation.org/model-minority.shtml

23   "2015 Statistical Portrait of Asian Americans, Native Hawaiians, and Other Pacific Islanders." UCLA Asian American Studies Center, 2015. http://www.aasc.ucla.edu/cic/stats2015.aspx

24   "Chapter 1: Portrait of Asian Americans." in "The Rise of Asian Americans." Washington, DC: Pew Research Center, June 2012. http://pewsocialtrends.org/2012/06/19/chapter-1-portrait-of-asian-americans/

25   ibid.

26   Pew Research Center survey on Asian Americans. Washington DC: Pew Research Center, 2012. http://www.pewsocialtrends.org/asianamericans/

27   Le, C.N. "Pew Report on Asian Americans: A Cautionary Tale." *Asian-Nation*, July 24, 2012. http://www.asian-nation.org/headlines/2012/07/pew-report-asian-americans-a-cautionary-tale/

28   Lee, Wanda M. L. *An Introduction to Multicultural Counseling.* Taylor & Francis, 1999. 104. https://books.google.com/books?id=OJyki76ec-cC&lpg=PA104&pg=PA104#v=onepage&q&f=false

29   "Field Listing: Religions." *The World Factbook.* Washington DC: Central Intelligence Agency, 2013. https://www.cia.gov/library/publications/the-world-factbook/fields/2122.html

30   Miller, Jack. "Religion in the Philippines." Asia Society. http://asiasociety.org/education/religion-philippines

31   Bird, Warren. "Korea: Why So Many Megachurches?" *Outreach Magazine,* June 18, 2015. http://www.outreachmagazine.com/ideas/11955-why-so-many-megachurches-in-korea.html

32   Kim, Rebecca Y. *The Spirit Moves West: Korean Missionaries in America.* Oxford University Press, 2015. 25-28. https://books.google.com/books?id=ffBxBgAAQBAJ&lpg=PP1&pg=PA25#v=onepage&q&f=false

33   Blumberg, Antonia. "China On Track To Become World's Largest Christian Country By 2025, Experts Say." *The Huffington Post,* April 22, 2014. http://www.huffingtonpost.com/2014/04/22/china-largest-christian-country_n_5191910.html

34   "Asian Americans: A Mosaic of Faiths." Washington, DC: Pew Research Center, July 2012. http://www.pewforum.org/2012/07/19/asian-americans-a-mosaic-of-faiths-overview/

35   Multiple sources for data cited in footnotes at http://multiasian.church/data/number-of-churches/

36   Carlson, Ken. "Models of Ministry in Chinese Churches." May 2007. http://kencarlson.org/series/chinese-church/models-of-ministry-in-chinese-churches/

37   Eng, Daniel K. "Asian American Church Models." July 2013. https://aapastor.wordpress.com/church-models/

38   See the 2 books published by Zondervan in the Leadership Network Innovation Series, *Multi-Site Church Revolution: Being One Church in Many Locations* and *Multi-Site Church Road Trip: Exploring the New Normal,* by Geoff Surratt, Greg Ligon, and Warren Bird.

39   Lee, Helen. "Silent Exodus: Can the East Asian church in America reverse the flight of its next generation?" *Christianity Today,* August 12, 1996. http://www.christianitytoday.com/ct/1996/august12/6t9050.html

40   Lee, Helen. "The Many Models of the Asian American Church: Once largely monocultural, Asian Americans' churches are now as diverse as the country they call home." *Christianity Today*, October 9, 2014. http://www.christianitytoday.com/ct/2014/september-web-only/many-models-of-asian-american-church.html

41   http://l2foundation.org/2009/books-by-l2-foundation

42   Chuang, DJ. "9 Things About Asian American Christianity." *The Exchange: A Blog by Ed Stetzer*, November 7, 2013. http://www.christianitytoday.com/edstetzer/2013/november/9-things-about-asian-american-christianity.html

43   "Number of Asian American Churches in the USA." *multiasian.church.* http://multiasian.church/data/number-of-churches/

44   Roach, David. "Page Receives Asian American Advisory Council Report." SBC LIFE, June 2015. http://www.sbclife.net/Articles/2015/06/sla10

45   Chuang, DJ. "Asian American Churches: An Introductory Survey." Dallas, TX: Leadership Network, 2009. http://l2foundation.org/2009/published-reports

46   http://djchuang.com/church-directory/next-gen-multi-asian-churches/

47   Narayanan, V.K. and Gina Colarelli O'Connor, eds. *Encyclopedia of Technology and Innovation Management.* John Wiley & Sons, 2010. On page 89, the original wording is, "a change that creates a new dimension of performance."

48   Brown, Brené. Listening to shame. TED video, 13:31, filmed March 2012. https://www.ted.com/talks/brene_brown_listening_to_shame

49   For additional considerations about next generation Asian Americans, see these recommended articles: Dr. Timothy Tseng's 2011 presentation, "Five Cries of Asian American Christian Young Adults" https://timtseng.net/2011/03/07/five-cries-of-asian-american-christian-young-adults-resource/, "The Young Adult Black Hole" https://timtseng.net/2011/09/01/the-young-adult-black-hole/, and Dr. Jerry Z. Park and Joshua Tom, "Keeping (and Losing) Faith, the Asian American Way." AAPI *Voices Project*, May 22, 2014. http://aapivoices.com/keeping-losing-faith/

50   Ray Chang's presentation, "East Meets West: Asian American Church Planting" at Exponential East, Orlando, April 27, 2015. http://regenerant.org/bonus-session-at-exponential-east-2015/

51   Penstone, James. "Visualising the Iceberg Model of Culture." *OpenGecko*, March 2011. http://opengecko.com/interculturalism/visualising-the-iceberg-model-of-culture/

52   http://djchuang.com/2014/being-asian-american-is-more-not-less/

53   Mosaic Church's diversity is about 15% white, 30% black, 20% Hispanic, and the rest are Asian and others, according to this article, "Mosaic: A church home for 'outsiders'." *Arkansas TImes*, July 24, 2008. http://www.arktimes.com/arkansas/mosaic-a-church-home-for-outsiders/Content?oid=868439

54   "The Theology of Multi-Ethnic Church: Diversity isn't just a social issues, it's a biblical one." *Leadership Journal*, June 2010. http://www.christianitytoday.com/le/2010/june-online-only/theology-of-multi-ethnic-church.html

55   Lipka, Michael. "Many U.S. congregations are still racially segregated, but things are changing." *Fact Tank*, Pew Research Center, December 8, 2014. http://www.pewresearch.org/fact-tank/2014/12/08/many-u-s-congregations-are-still-racially-segregated-but-things-are-changing-2/

56   Keller, Timothy. *Preaching: Communicating Faith in an Age of Skepticism.* Viking, 2015. 102.

57   https://twitter.com/timkellernyc/status/316280392372064256

58   Chuang, DJ. "Churches dying with dignity and recycling." *djchuang.com*, February 23, 2011. http://djchuang.com/2011/churches-dying-with-dignity-and-recycling/

59   Ziettlow, Amy. "Religion Runs in the Family." *Christianity Today.* September 20, 2013. http://www.christianitytoday.com/ct/2013/august-web-only/religion-runs-in-family.html

60   *Jimmy Kimmel Live*, 6:30, September 9, 2011. https://www.youtube.com/watch?v=vfet9cZO3vs

61   "Number of Jobs Held in a Lifetime." *National Longitudinal Survey FAQs.* Bureau of Labor Statistics, April 2016. http://www.bls.gov/nls/nlsfaqs.htm#anch41

62   Godin, Seth. *Linchpin: Are You Indispensable?* New York: Portfolio, 2011. 222.

63   Tokunaga, Paul. *Invitation to Lead: Guidance for Emerging Asian American Leaders.* InterVarsity Press, 2003.

64   Im, Daniel. "Campus Pastor Skill #3: How to Lead Down." September 6, 2016. <http://www.danielim.com/2016/09/06/campus-pastor-skill-3/>

65   "Annual Estimates of the Resident Population by Sex, Race Alone or in Combination, and Hispanic Origin." U.S. Census Bureau, Population Division, June 2016. http://factfinder.census.gov/bkmk/table/1.0/en/PEP/2015/PEPSR5H?slice=Year~est72015

66   U.S. Census projects the Asian American population will be 42.1 million by 2050, cf. Chapter 1 of this book.

67   http://archive.wired.com/science/discoveries/news/2006/06/71153?currentPage=all

68   thehomelessguy.wordpress.com

69   Tomkins, Stephen Michael. *The Clapham Sect: How Wilberforce's circle changed Britain.* Oxford: Lion Hudson, 2010.

70   From http://www.aspenideas.org/content/about: "The Aspen Ideas Festival is the nation's premier, public gathering place for leaders from around the globe and across many disciplines to engage in deep and inquisitive discussion of the ideas and issues that both shape our lives and challenge our times."

71   From https://www.weforum.org/about/world-economic-forum: "The Forum engages the foremost political, business and other leaders of society to shape global, regional and industry agendas."

72   From renaissanceweekend.org: For 35+ years, Renaissance Weekends—inter-generational, invitation-only retreats for preeminent authorities and emerging leaders—have celebrated both ideas and relationships: The continually revitalized "grand-daddy of ideas festivals," spawning countless friendships, ventures & initiatives.

73   https://en.wikipedia.org/wiki/TED_(conference)

74   Hochman, David. "No, His Name Is Not Ted: Chris Anderson, Curator of TED Talks, Builds his Brand." *New York Times*, March 7, 2014. http://www.nytimes.com/2014/03/09/fashion/Chris-Anderson-Curator-of-TED-Talks-Builds-his-Brand.html

75   Graham, Ruth. "Is It Too Late for Evangelical Christians to Honestly Discuss Same-Sex Marriage? A dispatch from this year's Q Ideas conference, or the Christian TED Talks." *Slate*, April 29, 2015. http://www.slate.com/articles/life/faithbased/2015/04/q_ideas_conference_2015_how_does_the_christian_ted_talks_deal_with_same.html

76   The Philanthropy Hall of Fame. http://www.philanthropyroundtable. org/almanac/hall_of_fame

77   To debunk other myths about philanthropy, read the article "Seven Myths about the Great Philanthropists" in *Philanthropy Roundtable* at http://www.philanthropyroundtable.org/topic/excellence_in_ philanthropy/seven_myths_about_the_great_philanthropists

78   From http://thegathering.com: "We are a group of individuals, families and foundations interested in Christian philanthropy. We serve as a resource to you, as well as a source of spiritual encouragement and a sounding board of peers."

79   Wang, Ruth. "Three Challenges Chinese Churches Facing: Theological Training, Open Preaching on Money, Cooperative Spirit." *China Christian Daily*, August 5, 2016. http://chinachristiandaily.com/2016-08-05/ church/three-challenges-chinese-churches-facing--theological- training--open-preaching--cooperative-spirit_2048.html

80   Laurie, Greg. "Money and Motives." *Harvest Daily Devotion*, April 19, 2008. https://www.harvest.org/devotions-and-blogs/daily- devotions/2008-04-19

81   "Jesus' Teaching on Money." *Preaching Today*, 1996. http://www. preachingtoday.com/illustrations/1996/december/410.html

82   "Historic $12 Million Gift Supports New Science Building." *The Campaign for Biola University Blog*, May 9, 2015. http://giving.biola.edu/news/2015/may/9/historic-12-million-gift/

83   Chuang, DJ. "Ethnicity, Context, and Mission: A Brighter Future for the Church." *The Exchange: A Blog by Ed Stetzer*, November 21, 2013. http://www.christianitytoday.com/edstetzer/2013/november/brighter- future-for-american-evangelical-church.html

84   Choung, James. "A New Frontier." INHERITANCE *Magazine*, December 2012. Retrieved from https://web.archive.org/web/20140701175714/ http://inheritancemag.com/cover-stories/a-new-frontier/1327. Aside: INHERITANCE Magazine <inheritancemag.com> was launched in 2009 to tell "stories about how Christian faith interacts with Asian and American cultures."

85   William Strauss and Neil Howe, *Generations: The History of America's Future*, 1584 to 2069, Quill, 1992. 415.

86   Adapted from a blog post by author titled, "Being Asian American is more not less" at djchuang.com, January 9, 2014. http://djchuang. com/2014/being-asian-american-is-more-not-less/

87   Kunkle, Brett. "How Many Youth are Leaving the Church?" *ConversantLife.com*, February 2009. http://www.conversantlife.com/theology/how-many-youth-are-leaving-the-church

88   Stafford, Tim. "The Tiger in the Academy: Asian Americans populate America's elite colleges more than ever—and campus ministries even more than that," *Christianity Today*, April 2006. http://www.christianitytoday.com/ct/2006/april/33.70.html

89   Also see Rebecca Y. Kim's essay, "Asian Americans for Jesus: Changing the Face of Campus Evangelicalism" Published February 2007 at Religious Engagements of American Undergraduates of the Social Science Research Council http://religion.ssrc.org/reforum/

90   Diversity statistics retrieved from https://www.cappex.com, unless otherwise indicated.

91   Yen, Hope. "Census: Whites no longer a majority in US by 2043." *Associated Press*, December 12, 2012. http://bigstory.ap.org/article/census-whites-no-longer-majority-us-2043

92   "Most Children Younger Than Age 1 are Minorities, Census Bureau Reports." U.S. Census Bureau, May 17, 2012. http://www.census.gov/snewsroom/releases/archives/population/cb12-90.html

ANNOTATED BIBLIOGRAPHY

This book was written rather concisely to make it an easier read for busy church leaders and pastors, so that readers can get a quick overview of the many opportunities and recognize the potential of next generation Asian Americans.

A good number of books have been published in recent years that do provide more in-depth research, insights, and perspectives for specific contexts within the broadly diverse Asian American population. This annotated bibliography is far from comprehensive, but serves as a starting point for further study. To refrain from giving my personal commentary and bias, I am presenting these annotations directly from each of their respective product description, adapted for brevity of length.

Please also refer to the additional resources published online at multiasian.church/resources that will be regularly updated.

Shin, Benjamin C. and Sheryl Takagi Silzer. *Tapestry of Grace: Untangling the Cultural Complexities in Asian American Life and Ministry*. Wipf and Stock, 2016.
> "Why do the first generation still act like that?" "Why are the second generation so disrespectful?" "Isn't it a shame how the church is split between the two generations?" These and many more questions reflect the tangled conflicts within the Asian American church. Cultural differences have led to many misunderstandings and conflicts. Conflicts have created bitterness and churches have split apart. How can these tangled threads be rewoven into a beautiful tapestry of God's grace? What would it take for the Asian American church to reflect God's grace? The co-authors apply their years of study and teaching to explain how the cultural complexities that occur between the different generations of the Asian American church can be untangled and how each generation can experience the amazing grace of the Gospel.

Park, M. Sydney Park, Soong-Chan Rah, and Al Tizon, eds. *Honoring the Generations: Learning with Asian North American Congregations.* Judson Press, 2012.

> In this intentionally grounded and richly theological volume, the editors bring together diverse leaders from pulpit and academy alike to explore the opportunities for ministry in an Asian North American Christian community that is increasingly challenged by a generation gap, not so much between age groups but between first-generation immigrants and the second- and third-generations. Contributors include Peter Cha, John Chung, Mitchell Kim, Sam Kim, David Lee, Grace May, Nancy Sugikawa, Gideon Tsang, Tim Seng, Jonathan Wu, Greg Yee, and Peter Yi.

Nakka-Cammauf, Viji and Timothy Tseng, eds. *Asian American Christianity: A Reader.* PAACCE & ISAAC, 2009.

> This textbook is an interdisciplinary collection of scholarly and religious articles about Asian American Christianity. Its four sections—contexts, sites, identity, and voices—offer in-depth understanding of both Catholic and Protestant traditions, practices, theologies, and faith communities. It also highlights diversity and complexity across lines of gender, generation, denomination, race, and ethnicity in Asian American Christianity.

Toyama-Szeto, Nikki, Tracey Gee, and Jeanette Yep, eds. *More Than Serving Tea: Asian American Women on Expectations, Relationships, Leadership And Faith.* InterVarsity Press, 2006.

> Asian American women are caught between different worlds. Many grew up sensing that daughters were not as valuable as sons. Family expectations and cultural stereotypes assume that Asian American women can only have certain prescribed roles, as if our worth comes only through what we do for others. But God has good news for Asian American women. In his eyes, they are his beloved daughters, created for greater purposes than the roles imposed upon us. In this one-of-a-kind book, a team of Asian American women share how God has redeemed their stories and helped them move beyond cultural and gender constraints. With the help of biblical role models and modern-day mentors, these women have discovered how God works through their ethnic identity,

freeing them to use their gifts and empowering them to serve and lead. Contributors include Asifa Dean, Christie Heller de Leon, and Kathy Khang.

Cha, Peter, S. Steve Kang, and Helen Lee, eds. *Growing Healthy Asian American Churches*. InterVarsity Press, 2006.
   The Asian American church is in transition. Congregations face the challenges of preserving ethnic culture and heritage while contextualizing their ministry to younger generations and the unchurched. Many Asian American church leaders struggle with issues like leadership development, community dynamics and intergenerational conflict. But often Asian American churches lack the resources and support they need to fulfill their callings. This book offers eight key values for healthy Asian American churches. Contributors include Nancy Sugikawa, Steve Wong, S. Steve Kang, Jonathan Wu, Paul Kim, Dihan Lee, Grace May, and Soong-Chan Rah.

Jeung, Russell. *Faithful Generations: Race and New Asian American Churches*. Rutgers University Press, 2004.
   Religion—both personal faith and institutional tradition—plays a central role in the lives of Asian Americans. It provides comfort and meaning, shapes ethical and political beliefs, and influences culture and arts. This book details the significance of religion in the construction of Asian American identity. As an institutional base for the movement toward Asian American panethnicity, churches provide a space for theological and political reflection and ethnic reinvention. With rich description and insightful interviews, the author uncovers why and how Chinese and Japanese American Christians are building new, pan-Asian organizations with unique pan-Asian styles of worship, ministries, and church activities.

Tokunaga, Paul. *Invitation to Lead: Guidance for Emerging Asian American Leaders*. InterVarsity Press, 2003.
   "The nail that sticks out gets hammered down." This Japanese expression characterizes the attitude of many Asian Americans. We are often taught not to put ourselves forward—not to stick out. But the Western concept of leadership is all about stepping up and standing apart from the group. Is that appropriate for Asian

Americans? Or can we lead out of our own cultural strengths rather than being pressed into the Western mold? Paul Tokunaga has been a ministry leader in Asian American, white and multiethnic contexts for many years. In this book, he offers, with surprising transparency, lessons from his own rich experiences—both successes and failures.

Fong, Kenneth Uyeda. *Pursuing the Pearl : A Comprehensive Resource for Multi-Asian Ministry.* Judson Press, 1999.

This book is an updated revision of the author's previously publication adapted from his doctoral dissertation about the legitimacy of Americanized Asian American ministries. This book speaks to nearly every generation of Asian North Americans who have a stake in the future of the church. Fong brings scholarly expertise and an in-depth knowledge of the cultural needs of more acculturated Asian North Americans and how to facilitate more effective ministry in Asian American churches.

Yep, Jeanette, Peter Cha, Susan Cho Van Riesen, Greg Jao, and Paul Tokunaga. *Following Jesus Without Dishonoring Your Parents.* InterVarsity Press, 1998.

Go to the right school. Become a doctor or a lawyer. Marry a nice Asian. These are some of the hopes of our Asian parents. Knowing that our parents have sacrificed for us, we want to honor their wishes. But we also want to serve Jesus, and sometimes that can seem to conflict with family expectations. Discovering our Asian identity in the midst of Western culture means learning to bridge these and other conflicting values. This book gives practical counsel on respect for parents, performance pressures, marriage and singleness, spirituality, and the unique gifts Asians bring to Western culture. The authors' ideas for living out the Christian faith between two cultures show us the way to wholeness.

INDIAN AMERICAN

George, Sam. *Understanding the Coconut Generation: Ministry to the Americanized Asian Indians*. Mall Publishing, 2006.
> Welcome to the brave new world of the second generation Indian Americans. Coconut is a metaphor for the emerging generation of Asian Indians in the Western societies. This book is about helping the coming generation of Asian Indians in North America to discover their unique identity, embrace their biculturalism, identify their spirituality, recognize their search for authentic community and empathize with some of their common struggles.

CHINESE AMERICAN

Yang, Fenggang. *Chinese Christians in America: Conversion, Assimilation, and Adhesive Identities*. Penn State University Press, 1999.
> As Christianity has become the most practiced religion among the Chinese in America, this book explores how Chinese Christians construct and reconstruct their identity—as Christians, Americans, and Chinese. There are more than one thousand Chinese churches in the United States, most of them Protestant evangelical congregations, bringing together diasporic Chinese from diverse origins—Taiwan, Hong Kong, mainland China, and Southeast Asian countries. Amidst many tensions, most individuals find ways to creatively integrate their evangelical Christian beliefs with traditional Chinese (mostly Confucian) values. The church becomes a place where they can selectively assimilate into American society while simultaneously preserving Chinese values and culture.

KOREAN AMERICAN

Kim, Sharon. A *Faith Of Our Own: Second-Generation Spirituality in Korean American Churches*. Rutgers University Press, 2010.
> Second-generation Korean Americans, demonstrating an unparalleled entrepreneurial fervor, are establishing new churches with a goal of shaping the future of American Christianity.

This book investigates the development and growth of these houses of worship, a recent and rapidly increasing phenomenon in major cities throughout the United States. By harnessing religion and innovatively creating hybrid religious institutions, second-generation Korean Americans are assertively defining and shaping their own ethnic and religious futures. Rather than assimilating into mainstream American evangelical churches or inheriting the churches of their immigrant parents, second-generation pastors are creating their own hybrid third space—new autonomous churches that are shaped by multiple frames of reference.

Kim, Rebecca Y. *God's New Whiz Kids?: Korean American Evangelicals on Campus.* NYU Press, 2006.

In the past 20 years, many traditionally white campus religious groups have become Asian American. Today there are more than fifty evangelical Christian groups at UC Berkeley and UCLA alone, and 80% of their members are Asian American. At Harvard, Asian Americans constitute 70% of the Harvard Radcliffe Christian Fellowship, while at Yale, Campus Crusade for Christ is now 90% Asian. This book focuses on second-generation Korean Americans, who make up the majority of Asian American evangelicals, and explores the factors that lead college-bound Korean American evangelicals—from integrated, mixed race neighborhoods—to create racially segregated religious communities on campus. Kim illuminates an emergent "made in the U.S.A." ethnicity to help explain this trend, and to shed light on a group that may be changing the face of American evangelicalism.

MULTIETHNIC

DeYmaz, Mark and Harry Li. *Leading a Healthy Multi-Ethnic Church: Seven Common Challenges and How to Overcome Them.* Zondervan, 2013.

Increasingly, church leaders are recognizing the power and beauty of the multi-ethnic church. Yet, more than a good idea, it's a biblical, first-century standard with far-reaching evangelistic potential. How can your church overcome the obstacles to become a healthy multi-ethnic community of faith? And why should you even try?

This book provides an up-close-and-personal look at seven common challenges to creating diversity in your church. Through real-life stories and practical illustrations, the authors show how to overcome the obstacles in order to lead a healthy multi-ethnic church. The book also includes the insights of other effective multi-ethnic church leaders from the United States and Australia.

Silzer, Sheryl Takagi. *Biblical Multicultural Teams*. William Carey International University Press, 2011.

Biblical Multicultural Teams speaks to the heart of cultural misunderstanding—our childhood upbringing. The author provides both an honest look at her own cross-cultural experience and an astute academic understanding of cross-cultural communication. We all work and function in a multicultural world. The advice and wisdom in this book will thus enable you to take a hard look at assumptions and attitudes found in your team and to work on submitting them to biblical standards of interaction.

Rah, Soong-Chan. *Many Colors: Cultural Intelligence for a Changing Church*. Moody Publishers, 2010.

The United States is currently undergoing the most rapid demographic shift in its history. By 2050, white Americans will no longer comprise a majority of the population. Instead, they'll be the largest minority group in a country made up entirely of minorities, followed by Hispanic Americans, African Americans, and Asian Americans. Past shifts in America's demographics always reshaped the county's religious landscape. This shift will be no different. This book is intended to equip evangelicals for ministry and outreach in our changing nation. Borrowing from the business concept of "cultural intelligence," the author explores how God's people can become more multiculturally adept. From discussions about cultural and racial histories, to reviews of case-study churches and Christian groups that are succeeding in bridging ethnic divides, Rah provides a practical and hopeful guidebook for Christians wanting to minister more effectively in diverse settings.

39961446R00093

Made in the USA
Middletown, DE
30 January 2017